A VERY

DIFFERENT WAR

A VERY DIFFERENT WAR

THE STORY OF AN EVACUEE
SENT TO AMERICA
DURING WORLD WAR II

BASED ON
LETTERS WRITTEN AT THE TIME

Louise Milbourn

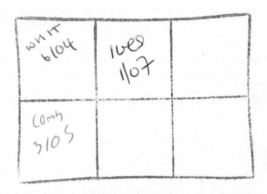

PRIVATELY PRINTED

First published in Great Britain
2003 by Isis Publishing Ltd

This edition published by Louise Milbourn 2004
Elmwood, Cuckoo Lane, Lolworth, Cambridge CB3 8HF

ISBN 0 95470 320 0

Designed and produced in 11/12pt Columbus by Geoff Green Book Design, Cambridge
Printed in Great Britain by Antony Rowe, Chippenham SN14 6LH

Frontispiece
Picture from a Philadelphia paper, August 1940
*"'English Refugees Here for War's Duration': Eight children of Quaker famlies arrived in the city
yesterday to be 'adopted' by families in this area, and here are two of them – Loiuse Lawson, 8, left,
and her sister, Blanche, 10 – standing amid their baggage and knapsacks at the 30th St. Station.
They will live with. Mr. and Mrs. Richard Wood, in Moorestown, N. J. "*

To my sister Blanche

Contents

Acknowledgements

I F IT HAD NOT BEEN for the letters this story would not have
been written. Found in my mother's attic the letters reveal the events
that my sister Blanche Sayers and I lived through from 1940–1945
in Moorestown, New Jersey. They bring an immediacy to the story
which my memory alone could not have done.

My first thanks go to Dick and Nancy Wood for taking us in and
making us part of their family without prejudice and relaying our lives
through letters to Plymouth, England. Likewise Rebecca, Anne and
Richard Wood accepted us as siblings into their household and made us
one of them. They have been helpful throughout in refreshing memories
and telling me how it was for them and allowing me to use the letters
freely.

Equally, Blanche to whom I dedicate this book has been most generous in the help and advice she has given, the use of her letters as well as
the title "A Very Different War". My brother John Lawson helped in
telling me his history back in England at this time.

There are others, descendants of letter writers, who I am indebted to
for allowing me to use their material. In England, Kenneth Major and
Joan Fox and in the U.S.A. Caroline Herrin, Henry Brown, his mother
and sister, Alison Senter and Megan and Dick Evans and Barbara Haas.

I am grateful for the discussions I had with Lilla Smithson and
Michael Rutter who sailed with me on the Duchess of Atholl to also stay
in Moorestown enabling me to compare experiences. I was glad in my
researches to meet by chance Roger Bennet and others who had sailed
on the Duchess of Athol when I did.

When it came to writing I could not have done without the help of the Cambridge U3A Writers Group who gently guided and encouraged my efforts ably lead by Elizabeth Bray who also took time to read and correct my script at what was a difficult time for her. Thanks too, to Phyllis Gibson for the use of her poem on Quaker meeting and the encouragement of her literary group.

My thanks to my son Andrew and his wife Jeanette for solving problems with my computer, my son Richard for his drawing of the Tobo embroidery and most importantly to my husband Graham who has been supportive and positive with helpful suggestions throughout.

CHAPTER ONE

The beginning

"**WHY DID THEY DO IT?**" That is the first question I am always asked. And what did they do? They were my parents and what they did was to send their two much loved little daughters, myself Louise and my elder sister Blanche, away from home, on our own, to stay with a family of total strangers 4000 miles away in a foreign land. One reply I frequently get from my contemporaries is: "Of course, I was going to go…" and the reasons would tumble out: "My parents changed their mind," "I was sent to Wales instead," or "The family decided to stick it out together". There was a lot of talk about escape from danger when many people were wondering what to do to escape from harm and here was I, someone who was sent away to safety.

We are talking of an earlier time, World War II, when the world was in a state of conflict and turmoil which had repercussions for so many people who lived through those years. Events that happened then would shape their lives. So it was for me. Decisions made then would change my life forever. There I was, eight years old, living a happy carefree country life in Devon with my parents, sister and brother before it all changed in the summer of 1940. I wonder if my mother and father realised the impact of the decisions they were making then. Our relationship one to another would, also, change forever. It would affect us all but probably my mother more than most.

There was more than one reason why our parents did this. At this time the War had been going on for nearly a year and the fear of an invading German army was on everyone's minds. It is difficult to explain, today, how real this fear was. Country after country across Europe had fallen to the advancing jackbooted army of Nazi Germany. Czechoslovakia, Poland, Norway, Holland, Belgium and even France had crumbled before the forces of Hitler's troops.

More compelling to my parents, living outside Plymouth, was the fact that by now Guernsey in the Channel Islands was already occupied as well. This was of great significance to my father, Francis Lawson, who had close ties with Guernsey. His mother was a Guernsey woman and he had spent many happy times as a boy visiting his many cousins on the island with whom he continued to be in touch. Prior to this invasion Guernsey had sent its women and children off the island scurrying to safer havens in Britain or further afield. Later, when tales were told of how those left behind fared for the next five years, there is no doubt that this had been a good decision. The deprivations and hardships were immense.

Another factor was the bombing that Plymouth was now receiving at the hands of the Luftwaffe. Plymouth harbour and its neighbour the Devonport dockyard were a vitally strategic military base, a large part of the Royal Navy was stationed here so from the beginning of the War the city had been a prime target and was to continue to be a prime target throughout hostilities. History bears this out. The centre of Plymouth had to be totally rebuilt afterwards.

I do not think this was the only matter that made my parents apprehensive. For two years before the outbreak of war in 1939 they had helped people fleeing from the oppressive Nazis in Europe. There had been a number of refugees, including Jews, from, Germany, Hungary, Poland and Czechoslovakia who had stayed in the house with us while they were looking for homes and employment in England. Many had worked for my father either in his Vineries (glasshouses) or on his farm because work on the land was acceptable. Would this mean that my parents would have been persecuted for this activity should the Germans arrive in Britain? It would certainly have been considered a major offence.

After much heart searching and much discussion the decision was made. In the way of Quakers, which my parents were, this decision would have been taken carefully making sure there was a consensus of feeling between them. Did they have any idea of the consequences of this decision? I and my sister were to be sent away from this threatened place to a place a long way away. For how long no one knew. My parents' fear was so great that they were prepared to split the family apart. My younger brother, John, too young to go, was left behind. Up to this time I had had an ordinary country childhood. What changes were to befall me.

After my mother died some years ago at the age of 92, having outlived my father by twelve years, the task then befell the family of clearing out the house. "Tobo", as it was called, was the only house my parents had ever lived in since their marriage of over 60 years before. It had been the background of my entire life

Tobo has an attic reached through a large trap door in the ceiling of the upstairs landing and entered by a ladder attached to the wall. It is a very large space extending over the whole house with a window in one gable end and room to stand in the centre under the roof ridge. Over the years it was the repository for all unwanted lumber and goods that somehow had avoided the dustbin or by some chance was thought might be wanted again in the future. A conglomeration of flotsam from the household. There were all manner of things from old television sets, boxes of tools and old ledgers and many suitcases and boxes with old photographs and papers. It even included a box with my grandfather's false teeth! Were they to be used again in the future? We siblings and our spouses worked our way through it all not sure what would be found next.

Suddenly Blanche gave a cry of wonder. "Look what this is. It's full of old letters. My goodness, it's the letters Aunt Nancy wrote to Mother during the War." (There were over 200 letters in all.)

"Why did she never tell us she kept them?"

I wondered. I am still wondering. We sat down and started reading. It brought the memories flooding back.

"What on earth shall we do with them? They have a real story to tell."

And that is how this book began.

CHAPTER TWO

Preparing to go

S O T H E D E C I S I O N to send us was made, but to where was
not. Various leads were taken up. One possibility had been to
join Dora Dorey, the wife of one of my father's cousins who,
having already escaped from the Channel Islands, was planning to take
her family to her brother, Kenneth Jackson, in Toronto. Two letters of
14th July 1940 from my father tell the story; one to Kenneth Jackson
and the other to his friend, a Mr. Mitchell both in Toronto.

Tobo,
Elburton,
Devon

14th July 1940

Dear Mr. Mitchell,

Kenneth Jackson has been good enough to arrange for you to take our daughter,
Louise. I wish to thank you for this most generous offer. Even if we are able to
repay you in money at some future date the very nature of your offer makes it
quite impossible to repay it in full. The only way in which it can be repaid to
you at present is by any enjoyment you will receive by having Louise with you
at your home. During the last year we have had many refugees from Central
Europe staying at our home and their friendship has been the best repayment
for our trouble.

It is difficult for a parent to sum up his own child. Louise is an affection-
ate child full of vitality, and I think one can say she has a sense of humour.
She is a child that people seem to enjoy. She likes games and gymnastics, loves

climbing trees and bathing, although she only swims a few strokes, she works very hard to become a better swimmer. She likes reading and needlework and is fairly good with her hands.

If I were able to send her under suitable conditions and she is able to get to Canada I trust that you will enjoy having her with you.

Yours sincerely,
Francis Lawson

Were they really going to send me on my own? I was shocked to read this years later. How glad I am that suitable conditions never materialised. For me, the younger of two girls, the essential feature of my evacuation when it came was that my older sister, Blanche, was with me and cared for and protected me.

The other letter written that same day went to Dora's brother and is more revealing of my parents' state of mind.

Tobo
Elburton
Devon

14th July 1940

Dear Kenneth Jackson,

Please accept my most sincere thanks for the offers you have made and found for my family; I feel you have undertaken more than you should out of the kindness of your heart and loyalty to Dora.

The position here is somewhat uncertain, owing to transport. The Government Scheme has been postponed. Just at present my wife, Joan, wishes to stay here with John for the time being and we are considering sending Blanche and Louise with Dora and your Mother and Father.

I was very anxious that Dora should put the word Quaker in her cable as you are no doubt aware we take a rather pacifist view of things and there are many who would not wish to take the child of a Quaker. I did not wish this fact to get you into any difficulty with your friends who are helping in this matter.

As the position of transport is so difficult I must ask your patience if we seem to hesitate on this side.

My wife and I can only offer our thanks at this time. But hope at some future date we may be able to repay you in kind. It is impossible ever to repay you in full as generosity is not a thing that can be repaid for in money.

Yours sincerely,
Francis Lawson

These letters reveal my father's personality in subtle ways. He was always someone who could understand another's point of view and also extremely honest. It would have been important to him that anyone taking on his lively eight year old daughter should be aware of the drawbacks that Quakerism might create. His membership of the Society of Friends or Quakers as they are frequently known, was important to him. He had not been born a Friend, as my Mother had, but had joined after attending a Quaker School even though his own parents were staunch Methodists.

My father who had a quiet sympathetic nature with a gentle sense of humour could get on with all kinds of people with great ease. To look at he was of medium height and slim build, with brown eyes hidden behind horn rimmed glasses, dark hair and dark complexion; colouring I had inherited. He was not particularly articulate nor did writing come easily so I feel sure my mother may have helped him compose this correspondence. Later, I would witness this kind of collaboration taking place. It is possible that signs of dyslexia would have been identified if he were at school now-a-days. But for anyone, what letters to write. Planning the departure of his two young daughters to strangers connected by the most tenuous links; the friend of the brother of the wife of a cousin.

We never got to Toronto. The suitable conditions were totally wrecked by an outbreak of measles among Dora's five children. We literally missed the boat. Another offer came, this time from two unmarried ladies in Rhode Island; but this was deemed inappropriate.

It would appear that my parents were very set on finding a home for us overseas at whatever cost. Was the fear of an invasion and the possible consequences for them as the result of helping the refugees, the enemies of the Third Reich, sufficiently serious for this course of action to be taken? Were their names on the Nazi "hit list" that came to light after the War was over? They never mentioned this as a reason for their actions but perhaps it was in the back of their minds at the time.

Eventually an appropriate organisation arose which linked the American Committee for the Evacuation of Children with the Central Offices of the Society of Friends (Quakers). This time the "rather pacifist view of things" would not be a disadvantage and the arrangements would enable Quaker children to go to Quaker families in the United States. At last! A way to get the children away and this time, if they went to Friends with a large "F", our parents knew their standards and beliefs in life would be similar.

Official documents arrived from Friends House, London, the home of the central administration of the Society dated 30th July 1940. Among the information provided was the news that accommodation had been offered to Friends by the U.S. Committee for the care of European Children on a ship sailing about the middle of August, 1940 barely two weeks away. This was nearly one year after the outbreak of war between Britain and Germany.

The cost of the journey was £16, third class. Other details follow about the need for an engraved identity disc to be hung on a chain round the neck, the incidental expenses of the journey and application forms. We were to attend interviews at Friends House on Thursday 8th August.

Further instructions established the rules of this complicated operation.

> "Parents must be prepared to allow their children to be sent where accommodation is available, not to limit their application with burdensome conditions, nor to withdraw it when arrangements are otherwise complete. The full accommodation of the children must rest with Friends in the reception country and cannot be undertaken from this end."

A frenzy of preparation ensued to comply with all the instructions in the short time available. New clothes were bought and name tapes sewn on everything while I watched in wonder at all the activity. I am certain that I really had very little understanding of the implications of what was going on. In many ways I felt I was being prepared for an adventure and quite enjoyed being the centre of attention while the making ready was going on.

Letters of many friends of my parents showed their grave concern for my parents aware of the very great risks they were taking by sending their daughters so far away. Ships travelled in convoy, escorted by destroyers for greater safety. Nevertheless, the amount of shipping belonging to the Allies that had already been lost when crossing the Atlantic from September 1939 until June 1940 was 2,300,000 tons. Then in the following six months a further 2,500,000 tons were sunk, probably over 100 ships. The German U-boats (submarines) were creating havoc for all ships making the crossing of the Atlantic Ocean in the summer of 1940. It was an extremely dangerous place.

The interviews were duly attended and the following letter assuming our acceptance arrived.

CENTRAL OFFICES OF THE SOCIETY OF FRIENDS

Friends House
Euston Road
London, N.W.1
August 9th, 1940

EVACUATION OF CHILDREN
FINAL ASSEMBLY AND DEPARTURE ARRANGEMENTS

Dear Friend,
With regard to the interview which your children had yesterday with the American Consul I am directed by the American Committee for the Evacuation of Children to send you the following instructions. The children must attend on Monday 12th August, at Friends House between the hours of 3p.m. and 8p.m. for final instructions, tickets, passports, labels etc. They will then report to the Board Room, Grosvenor House, Park Lane, London, W.1. (entrance Upper Grosvenor Street) at 8a.m. on Tuesday August 13th. From Grosvenor

House they will proceed under the control of escorts and parents may not be
allowed to accompany the children beyond this point.
Yours sincerely,
Stephen Thorne

The final day, August 14th 1940 arrived. The same day as my mother's
birthday; a more poignant time for our leaving would be hard to find.
This departure date had been delayed two days for unknown reasons
but unexpected delays were commonplace during war time and people
learned to wait, they had no choice. We had passed the waiting hours
while in London visiting some of the sites such as St. Paul's Cathedral
and Buckingham Palace reminders we would take from the country
and culture of the England we were leaving behind.

CHAPTER THREE

Leaving

S UDDENLY THE EXCITEMENT of being in London dissipat-
ed and my sister and I found ourselves being checked in at the
board room of the Grosvenor House. A British passport valid for
U.S.A. and Canada, an American Visa, a bus voucher, a railway ticket, a
steamship ticket, a National Registration and Identity Card, and a ration
book all had to be ticked off for each child. Blanche and I already had
identity discs around our necks and the same details of name and
address sewn in our coats. All this had been checked and double
checked by our mother who was always meticulous in what she did.

Blanche
Passport photographs, August 1940

Louise

The instructions on 'The Essentials to be Worn on the Day of the Journey' had been very precise:

a Mackintosh to be carried on arm
b Gas Mask to be slung across right shoulder
c Haversack over left shoulder – containing:
   Overnight attire
   Minimum toilet requisites
   Sufficient food (sandwiches) and
   Thirst quenching drink for a long day.

We were taken to the ballroom to meet our escort, Miss Helen Andrews, a tall spinsterish woman who was to be responsible for our group of 15 children. We joined all the other groups with their escorts clustered on the ballroom floor. By now we had the look of refugees; clutching hand luggage and gas mask, labels on everything flapping and in the way, all herded together in a crowd. Then there was the increasing noise of crying children as they realised that the long journey was about to begin and the separation was starting. I like everyone else was totally bewildered.

It was here we had our last hugs and kisses but not our last sight of our mother. The parents were ushered out and then allowed upstairs on to the gallery of the ballroom where they could look down on this sea of now orphaned children. It appears they were actually locked in to stop any last minute dashes to the floor below to snatch a child, overcome by a change of heart.

"Blanche, can you see Mummy up there? I can't see her."

"There she is Louise, right up over there. There. Look."

"Where? Where? I still can't see her!"

"She had her blue hat on, you know, the one with those little feathers. See there."

"Oh yes, I can now. Wave."

"Oh, do be careful, Louise, you're going to lose your gas mask, stay near me and stop bobbing up and down so. Mummy has seen us now."

Mother's last words to Blanche had been, 'Look after Louise'. A heavy responsibility she would take very seriously and not easy for a ten year old. My tendency to bob about was going to be a problem.

Our mother was looking down through her tears on a chaotic scene of jostling children interspersed with anxious adults trying to keep some modicum of order. At last she could pick out her two girls with their identical berets, one pale blue and one pale yellow, and waved.

My mother, who looked down, was a very attractive woman with very blue eyes, a pale clear complexion, a central parting with long black hair pulled back in a chignon at the base of her neck. She dressed neatly and enjoyed pretty dresses and hats. This day it was the blue one with the small feathers. Quaker tradition was that one should not encourage vanity by wearing fashionable clothes to draw attention to yourself, historically Quakers were known for wearing plain grey in response to this. Even in the mid-20th Century this influence remained. This created a conflict for my mother which she found difficult to resolve because she rather enjoyed dressing smartly and being the centre of attention.

More on her mind at this moment was whether her girls would be safe. Would Miss Andrews be able to cope? Her sister Kitty hadn't been very encouraging. "The Friends surely have little perception of what's involved if they use a person like Helen Andrews for that job. Even her looks would be enough to put the children off, and she knows nothing of children," was Kitty's comment. Her clothes, about which Aunty Kitty was so disparaging included a range of saggy cardigans and jumpers worn over rather shapeless skirts. One jumper Blanche remembers with horror. It was bright green with a very intricate lacy pattern, home knitted with much effort, but the horror was you could see her underwear underneath through the holes! Mother could do nothing about the choice of escort and just hoped all would go well.

This was the last view I had of my mother as I was shepherded out by Miss Andrews to embark on our journey to our new life in the New World. It was to be five whole years almost to the day before we would see England again. Later Mother said she had no idea our separation would be for such a very long time. She wondered many times if she and my father would have made the same decision had they known it was to be so very long and have had to sacrifice seeing their daughters grow up. The heartbreak of saying goodbye would have compounded the distress if she had known this then.

Many years later I found myself in the ballroom of the Grosvenor House Hotel, this time attending a very grand Farmer's Club Ball where elegant ladies in colourful taffeta ball gowns and men in formal evening wear were dancing to the melodies of a twelve piece band. To begin with I did not realise where I was until down on the dance floor I looked up and saw the gallery above.

"Oh my goodness! This was the place," I said to my husband with whom I was dancing.

"What place?" he asked.

"The place where I said good bye to my mother before embarking on my journey to America in 1940. What a different scene it was then."

I'm glad to say I could not hear the cries of the children above the rhythm of the band that night.

The consolation for my parents was that I and my sister would be safe with Mr. and Mrs. Linton and family in Moorestown, New Jersey. The news of where we were to go had already been received and the place had been found on the map to be not far from Philadelphia. The dangers of being at home in Devon were by now quite evident in the frequent bombing being meted out to Plymouth, so near us.

By the time I left, I had experienced nights in the air raid shelter and watched in awe at the searchlights swinging over the city sky creating a pattern of light beams many times more dramatic than the laser lights of a *son et lumière* one might see today. I can remember seeing those beams penetrating the darkness, sometimes lighting the grey floating monsters looking like legless elephants that were barrage balloons, suspended there to form a shield against the circling aeroplanes with their deadly load of bombs. As the lights swept back and forth you could sometimes catch sight of the glisten of light on metal identifying the fuselage of an aeroplane searching for the target of their bombs below. I could also see glimpses of the Spitfires chasing and harassing the bombers caught in the lights as they in turn sought their targets. It was very exciting to watch.

"Look, I can see," I would call, hopping up and down with excitement. "No, its gone, oh there it is again coming out from that cloud." I was gripped by the fever of the hunt.

One glimpse of that shine on metal was all that was needed to set the anti-aircraft guns stationed at Queen Anne's Battery into action as they in turn found their target. The noise was deafening.

Not surprisingly, I was not allowed to stand in the open and watch this battle of the skies but was hustled down to the air raid shelter and safety. The air raid shelter where we sought safety during these raids was dug in the Devon hedge that separated our house from my grandparents house next door. There was a difference in height between the two gardens so by digging under the hedge from my grandfather's, (Lealholm) side, it had meant less digging. It was not a very big shelter, just big enough to house some narrow bunks for us youngsters to sleep on and another for the adults to sit on. It was a dark damp place with the smell of damp earth and for my sister, Blanche, with her fear of spiders, a decidedly inhospitable place. During those first heavy raids I would be wrapped in a blanket late at night when the siren went and hustled down across the garden into this dark cellar place.

Mother would come into the bedroom I shared with my sister. "Come on, wake up. Wake up, Louise, the siren's gone."

"No, I don't want to, it's too cold."

"You must, you must. Come on, hurry, hurry."

The shelter had been placed so it could be shared with our grandparents but because Granny Lawson had had a stroke and was an invalid they never joined us. Instead they made other arrangements inside the house. There we stayed, my mother and her children waiting until the distant noises of explosions died away and the All Clear Signal sounded.

Later life became more organised and going to bed at night I had to have my dressing gown and slippers handy and ready to put on for the hurried exodus. Experience taught the adults to be more circumspect in deciding whether we had to go down to that hole in the ground because the raids could be centred further away right on the other side of town over Devonport, where the planes targeted the dockyard. If that was the case it was worth the risk of having an undisturbed night.

There was one terrible night after we had left when the raiding planes were to mistake the moonlight shining on the glasshouses of father's vineries for the waters of Sutton Pool in Plymouth Harbour and dropped the bombs close by.

Father would not be with us as he had joined the Fire Service and would be out in the danger trying to stem the damage caused by the incendiary bombs which could create nearly as much havoc as the explosives. For two reasons my father was not in one of the fighting services; firstly he was working in the glasshouse business which meant he was in a reserved occupation producing food and secondly because of his pacifist views he had registered as a Conscientious Objector. However, this did not stop him from taking part in this non-combatant activity.

CHAPTER FOUR

The journey

FOR MY MOTHER these experiences will have reminded her
that there was hope of safety for her two girls as she finally saw
them leave the ballroom. After all, it was because they came
from such a vulnerable area they had been included in this group of
children filing out.

As we left the Grosvenor House that late afternoon for myself and
Blanche this was the beginning of an adventure and ordeal in equal
parts. Blanche as eldest was trusted with two important letters given
to her by Mother to be given to our escort, Miss Andrews or any
other adult who was charged with our care during the journey. The
first from our doctor, who was a family friend and also a Friend, was
brief.

> *Bramley Tor*
> *Seymour Park*
> *Plymouth*
> *11.8.40*

*I have known Blanche and Louise Lawson since birth. (She had delivered
us at home at Tobo.) Blanche, I think, needs the greater attention as to
health; she is not so robust as Louise and is inclined to be of a highly strung
temperament. She is more backward in development and not so alert intellectually as Louise. Louise is more placid and independent. She is of a tom-boy
character and of a stronger physique. Blanche, I would imagine, to be more*

reserved and perhaps a type which would, therefore, fret more for her home
people. Blanche needs to be watched for any tendency to rheumatic pains.

Norah C. Goodbody, MB. ChB.

In the event the suggestion that Blanche would suffer homesickness
was proved wrong and quite unexpected. Poor Blanche is painted as a
somewhat fretful child but I think the adults underestimated her inner
strength in the face of the trials to come. She was an attractive girl with
a wide forehead, green eyes and pale complexion, and mousy straight
hair. The concern about rheumatics is very much a reflection of the
times when houses were not heated and often damp. Rheumatic fever,
which was not uncommon, was a debilitating illness that could leave
children handicapped for life and very much feared, as Infantile Paralysis was once we got to America.

The second was an open letter from my mother to explain the idio-
syncrasies of her daughters.

To Miss Andrews OR to Whom it May Concern
Dear Friend,

Some notes about our two daughters, Blanche and Louise, may be helpful in
your care of them during the coming journey to Albert Linton, Moorestown
New Jersey. The enclosed copy of their doctor's report may also be of guid-
ance: as far as it goes, it is correct.

Louise's exuberance is inclined to run away with her; her ability to climb
startles strangers, but she rarely comes to grief. She has always been allowed a
free hand in the matter. However, on a boat it will obviously have to be held in
check. In the same way, her capacity to cry loudly embarrasses those who do
not know her. On the other hand, she is more sensitive, affectionate and timid
than you would think.

Dr. Goodbody has not mentioned the fact that her stomach gets upset easily,
often for a nervous reason and she has already been discovered to be a bad
sailor. She responds well to Glucose D and water.

Blanche on the other hand, is well described by Dr. G. but there is one
trouble that is a very real worry and she needs definite help in it. She has what
one may call a Spider Phobia and we have been quite unable to cure it. Her

first reaction to any new building or room is to search it for spiders and she certainly cannot rest until they are removed; to her it is devastating and really not to be jeered at.

Could you kindly keep a watchful eye on her gold plate. She takes it out when bathing but has to be reminded to do so. She is a responsible child and both she and Louise are trustworthy. Blanche is also good at helping younger children than herself. Their general table manners are appalling and they are both thoroughly mischievous at times but I can't help that and doubtless others can cope better than I.

Their luggage has been labelled some to be used on journey and some that need not be touched. Blanche has Iodex for her legs if they pain her as they do if she gets really tired or over excited.

The things over which the Customs Official might be anxious are:

1. Blanche's gold metal plate, value 7 Guineas
2. Blanche's wristwatch, value £2
3. Louise's violin and case, value £3
I have told Blanche that they are to wear their older clothes on the journey.

Joan Lawson

The gold plate which was to have straightened my sister's teeth was a constant trial and she had a funny way of flopping it around in her mouth which could drive those around her crazy. It had been the centre of a dramatic incident a year earlier when on holiday on a Guernsey beach. Splashing and swimming in water just within her depth there was a sudden cry:

"I've dropped my plate! Help, help! I've dropped my plate," she shouted loudly.

Adults nearby were summoned to the rescue, at first thinking someone's life was in danger from the volume of the shouts.

"What is it?"

"Blanche has dropped her plate."

"Where? Where? Where were you when it happened?"

It took a half hour of diving and sifting sand but eventually father found it. No more swimming with the plate in, especially when 7 guineas

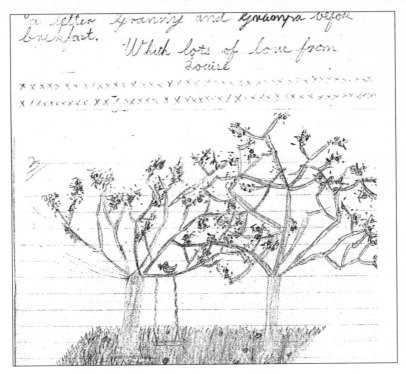

First letter home

was at stake, more than twice the value of a violin even a half sized one such as mine.

On the other hand, the predictions on my sea faring abilities proved to be quite correct as letters written on board the boat and posted in Montreal demonstrate.

My Dear Mummy and Daddy,
We had a very bad journey up to Liverpool from Euston. The train was sup-posed to go at 12 o'clock but it went at 1 o'clock, the Nichalls boy and another boy threw pillows at me but I did not wake up. I did not know they threw pil-lows at me till Blanche told me. Then we had all morning till we got on the boat and had dinner at 2 o'clock then had a rest. The next day I was sick four times and once in the night: on Sunday I had a tummyack so did not get up.

*But I got up on Monday. We have to carry our lifebelts every were we go on
the ship.*

*We see land to night and go threw the Gulf of St. Lawrence tomorrow on
Thursday we stop at Quebec for 7 hours some children may go on shore, they
are lucky if they do. We go down the river and due at Montreal on Friday.
And they say there is a heat-wave in New York.*

*I hope you like the picture I am sending you. Are daddy's apples like the
ones in the picture or arnt they ripe yet and a lot of windfalls or not. When I
drew the swing it made me think of daddy splicing the robes. Does John still
love the swing. Are the birds getting at Daddy's apples, the bird in my piture
has an apple in his beak. Give my love to John I better stop becace I hope I can
write a letter Granny and Grampa before brekfast.*

With lots of love from

Louise.

*XXXXXXXXXXXXXXXXXXXXXXXXXXXXXXXXXXXXXXXXXXXXXXX
XXXXXXXXXXXXXXXXXXXXXXXXXXXXXXXXXXXXXXXXXXXXXXX
XXXXXXXXXXXXXXXXXXXXXXXXX*

Dear Granny and Grampa,

*I hope Gran is getting better. We were caught in fog this morning so we may be
late in getting to Montreal. Tell mummy she should have put my E string in
because I want to play my violin in a consert on the boat. Blanche is going to
write something below. Whith love from Louise*

XXXXXXXXXXXXXXXXXXXXXXXXXXX XXXXX

Dear Grampa and Granny,

*We have been surprisingly well. I was only sick twice but Louise was sick five
times. Please will you tell Mummy that I have cracked the glass of my watch
because I forgot to put it in her letter.*

With love from Blanche

Please give my love to Nurse.

X X X X X X X X X X X X X X

*P.S. Since Louise and I wrote your letter we have seen six icebergs some big
some medium and some small.   Blanche and Louise*

What these letters do not convey was my bewilderment at everything that was happening. At eight years old all decisions about events had been made by adults over my head. So though I knew what was happening sufficiently to get through the days I can remember a certain sense of confusion as we were chivvied from one place to the next.

Nor does my letter describe how long the wait at Euston felt. It had been quite early in the evening when we arrived there. We were trapped in Euston Station by an air raid that prevented all trains from leaving. No air raid shelter this time, just herded together sitting on the dirty floor waiting and waiting. At that time of steam trains, stations were full of grime and soot, so our little band were getting more tired and grubbier as the clock slowly ticked the hours away. To help pass the time some enthusiastic adult led a sing-song. 'Roll Out the Barrel' and 'What Shall We Do With the Drunken Sailor' were two songs to which amazingly other people seemed to know the words. I certainly didn't feel like singing.

I was lucky to sleep on the overnight train journey despite the pillows aimed at me! Blanche remembers that it was the next morning I cried for my mother while being comforted on Miss Andrews' lap and she told me pragmatically that I couldn't have my Mummy now. I think I have blocked off a lot of this early part of the journey as too awful to even think about, the reality of no Mummy best forgotten.

We joined the "*Duchess of Athol*", one of 28 ships that made up the convoy, at Liverpool. She was not a large ship (20,000 tons) though it seemed like it to me. Like all ships she had long passageways running between the cabins, with stairs and companionways leading from deck to deck making it quite difficult to find your way without getting lost. The worst bit was a long difficult walk to the dining room, not helped by the rolling of the ship as it ploughed through the North Atlantic waves making the floor unsteady as you went.

As an adult I have this recurring nightmare. I am trying to find my way through a large building with many rooms, more staircases and more corridors and I can never find my way out. The buildings of my dreams are very varied and rarely the same but always that lost feeling in long corridors. Does this stem from that lost feeling below decks on the *Duchess of Athol*, dragging my orange lifebelt behind me?

Above decks it was not so alarming, my tomboy nature saw me climbing the rigging when the sailors' backs were turned and playing with the others in Miss Andrews' group.

Then as our ship moved north to enter the mouth of the St. Lawrence river we saw icebergs. We were being read a story by Miss Andrews when a lady came to say; "Have you seen the icebergs?" Of course we hadn't. So we all rushed up on deck to have a look.

"Oh, look, arn't they beautiful?"

We could see large pure white shapes of ice with blue shadows nearly as big or bigger than our vessel floating on the very blue sea.

Someone told us, "You are only seeing the very top of the block of ice, nine tenths is hidden under the water. If you go too close the ship can be wrecked on the hidden part underneath." The fate of the *Titanic* was still remembered.

Next it was the notorious fog of the Grand Banks. This slowed our speed down to the constant accompaniment of a mournful foghorn so by then we were reduced to being only one day ahead of schedule. No wonder there was relief on finally reaching our destination.

On landing in Montreal Miss Andrews quickly posted letters back to the parents of her charges.

Duchess of Athol
Nearing Quebec
Aug. 22, 1940

Dear Joan Lawson,

We are safe in the St. Lawrence and my 15 charges are well and bonny, Louise and Blanche have been ever so good and helpful, especially Blanche who often comes forward and helps with my babes.

They were both sick on the Day we christened "Black Saturday", in fact very few survived at all — only three in our set, besides myself. I was lucky, some escorts were ill themselves and had all their children down.

We were convoyed by a destroyer for 2¼ days — and it is still marvellous to be safe in the river and feel one can really sleep with impunity, our task nearly accomplished.

There are 1300 passengers of which 650 are children. I have loved my

chickens and have been christened Mrs. Disney by the other Escorts because we
always hunt together.
*   I am ever so sorry I've to hand them over at Montreal. I'd rather have fin-*
ished by taking them to New York.

Later
Safe in the Youth Hostel at Montreal. I am handing over to the American
Friends' Escort tomorrow morning, Sunday. Its been a record passage, 8 days.

Yours sincerely,
Helen Andrews

Miss Andrews had obviously managed better than my Aunty Kitty
could have predicted. Her letter does not fully describe the truly per-
ilous nature of that sea passage I am quite certain she did not wish to
alarm my parents. Only her evident over-whelming relief on arrival in
the St. Lawrence River lets one recognize how stressful the journey had
been. In the early stages of the voyage the convoy had travelled far
faster than usual, zigzagging as we went, gaining two days because we
were chased by U-boats and our destroyer escort had dropped depth
charges to protect us. They were that close!

Years later my sister met Jack Power, a man in the merchant navy
who had been one of the crew on the *Duchess of Athol*, who considered
that crossing the worst trip he made in the whole War. It was he who
told her something I did not know before which was that one night 11
ships were lost out of the convoy of 28. If we had gone down, none of
us would have survived despite the regular lifeboat drills we were sub-
jected to. He told how after that the *Duchess of Athol* broke convoy she
sailed on with one destroyer to the mouth of the St. Lawrence.

How lucky we were to get through! I was not to know then, only
years later, of the fate of the ship called the *City of Benares* just exactly
how lucky that was. A month after our crossing this ship, again full of
evacuees, was sunk with the loss of nearly everyone on board, only
seven children survived. After that no more children were evacuated to
America.

Playing my violin for the concert on the boat never happened because of the absence of the E string. But concert there was, held for the dignitaries of Montreal when we finally got there. We all had to sing the "Maple Leaf Forever", the Canadian National Anthem, having had the words of several verses drilled into us during the last days of the voyage as we sailed the calmer waters of the St. Lawrence River.

News of the safe arrival of the *Duchess of Athol* was received in England when an item on the 9 o'clock news on 23rd August 1940 reported that children from Britain had arrived at a port in Eastern Canada, some destined for homes in America. A letter to my mother from my Aunty Kitty sums up the mood back in England.

The Vicarage
Green Lane
Leigh
Lancs.
25th Aug. 1940

Dearest Joan,

I want to thank you now for your long lovely letter and the two phone calls. The letter will be one of those which are kept, for it is one of the ones dealing with a historic event in our family, and will go along with ones like Father's last letter to me, his letter on our engagement and so on. But the pathos in it, is a mark too, for you give such a detailed account of the four of you that anyone reading it must realise the poignancy of the human suffering in it and still know the world is good. I have lived these days with you in spirit, thinking of those two going out together to the big new world with brave little hearts, though withal unknowing. You must probably tell yourself that their homesickness and longing for you will soon pass and they adapt themselves to the new life and be happy in it especially, Louise.

Let us hope that the War will not last very much longer so that they may not grow too far away from you nor take on the American lingo too completely. How thrilled I was when I heard the news of their arrival and then your phone call right on top of it. What a relief to you.

Dearest love,

Kitty

CHAPTER FIVE

The home left behind

A T LAST SAFE IN MONTREAL the home I had left behind was still very much in my thoughts and my letters home always included lots of love and kisses for younger brother John, a full five years younger than me, the longed for son of the family. He was just three years old when I left and too small to be parted from his parents. He was a good natured happy smiling child with fair hair but still treated as a baby by his older sisters. Not quite big enough to keep up with our games and play but involved when it suited us.

Until I left I had had a happy middle class childhood centred on Tobo, my home just outside Plymouth in rural Devon. The house was built in 1928. It was designed by a cousin of my mother's during my parents engagement; no turning back with such a commitment. It was typical of houses built between the wars, particularly the metal framed crittal windows much used then. Virginia creeper climbed happily up the walls covering much of the front façade, going a lovely crimson in autumn. The house was built in a

Tobo. The Lawson family home

The fire screen embrodoidery (sketched by Richard Milbourn) showing Tobo and the Vineries

bare field next door to my grandfather Lawson's house that was soon planted with trees and my memory is of a garden full of trees, many of which I enjoyed climbing to the very top.

Tobo stood back from the road separated from it by a Devon hedge. This is a broad-based stone wall topped with earth on which trees and shrubs grow, making a considerable barrier between the house and passing traffic in the road. It formed a definite edge to my world up till then. The house stood in a slightly raised position with the best views facing north, thus from the bathroom you could see in the distance what looked like snow capped mountains, much to the amazement of visitors not expecting the Alps in Devon. The snow capped peaks were the white spoil heaps of the china clay workings on Dartmoor.

Inside the house there was an intentional cottagey feeling, bare wood floors with mats, wooden doors with black iron catches that were quite impossible to close quietly, nor would they shut on their own.

"Louise, don't slam the door. Louise, you are in too much of a hurry, shut it properly," the nearest adult would complain.

Besides the doors the mats could cause problems as well because they were liable to skid alarmingly on the polished floor, especially the one in the hall. Isaac Foot, the father of the political Foot Brothers, Hugh, Dingle, Michael, John and Christopher was known to have taken a skate on these; fortunately with no lasting injury. Towards the very end of her life when my mother was getting less stable on her legs she refused to allow the mats in the hall to be either anchored or removed. I think she wanted to convince herself she could still negotiate them even if her hapless visitors could not.

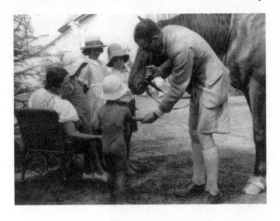

Feeding Tommy the family pony. Left to right. Mother, Blanche, two cousins, Louise (smallest) and Father

Much of the furniture in the house had been hand made in oak for my parents as newlyweds. Crafts and things handmade were very much a feature of Tobo; reminiscent of the Arts and Crafts movement. On the staircase were small wooden panels of animals carved by my father. My mother was also good with her hands and was a keen and accomplished embroiderer. A beautiful piece of work was the embroidered fire screen in pride of place in front of the grate showing a picture of Tobo and its environs, all done in drawn thread work. This was something I could recognise, this was my world. It showed Tobo and the garden, Lealholm, my grandparents' house next door, the field behind the house where Tommy the bay pony grazed and further away were the greenhouses of the Vineries and the fields at the farm called Dodovens with its orchards. The only thing it did not show was my grandfather's tool shop in Plymouth.

The fact that my mother, with three children, could spend time on intricate embroidery and not in the kitchen tells us of the kind of middle class life she led. Help in the house was available, often the wives of men who worked at the Vineries who would come to clean, cook and look after us.

I gather I had been quite a handful as a toddler, displaying all the difficulties of the "terrible twos". Florrie had been engaged to live in to

Louise and dolls, age 3, in front of Tobo

help cope with this sleepless toddler. Thus it was her task to try and quell the howls in the middle of the night. I got to love her dearly. She seemed quite grown up to me but she was only sixteen when she first arrived at Tobo, a very pretty girl with lovely fair curly hair. Besides looking after us children she was also expected to help in the house polishing floors and with the laundry, altogether a demanding job.

Before I went away she was being courted by the butcher's boy who arrived with parcels of meat from the village twice a week. Percy was tall, tall enough to chat through the quite high kitchen window with ease. Tall enough to delight John by tossing him high in the air.

"Me too!" I would beg, but sadly I was considered too big for such baby fun and games. It often took quite a long time for the parcel of meat to be handed over.

The Vineries where my father and grandfather worked was an extensive area of greenhouses where tomatoes, cucumbers, French beans and grapes were grown along Guernsey lines. Such an intensive growing process employed a large workforce probably around fifty men to do the skilled tasks involved. This made it one of the larger employers in the village of Elburton.

I considered it a great treat to visit the Vineries. I remember, particularly, the different smells of the different crops; the special astringent smell of the tomatoes climbing up wires forming a narrow alleyway along either side of the path with trusses of red or partly red fruit contrasting with the vivid green foliage. The cucumber house was a special favourite.

"Daddy, are you going to the Vineries? Can I come with you?" I would ask.

"All right, come along" my father would reply, "but don't get in the way."

"Are you going to look at the cucumbers?" I would ask.

"Yes, they're in Number 7 green-house this year."

"Oh, goodie!"

So I would hop along trying to keep up until we got to the greenhouse.

"Now, you must get through the door quickly and make sure you shut it behind you," Father would say. Oh dear, doors again. "You have to get through the door quickly to stop the expensive heat from escaping."

Once inside it was another world.

Louise with gosling

There was an extra hot steamy smell, the foliage lush dark green, grow-ing so tall it almost cut out the light so you could imagine you were walking in an equatorial forest. I was reminded of this smell years later on landing at Entebbe airport in Uganda in the middle of tropical Africa. The heat and smell of Africa greets you on the airport tarmac as soon as you walk down the steps of the aircraft just as it did on entering the cucumber house at the Vineries.

Besides working at the Vineries my father also worked on the 70 acres at Dodovens not far from where we lived. This was an enterprise of his own, separate from his father where he had planted apple orchards. I could just remember when the later fields were planted with trees, in lines whichever way you looked; ahead, sideways, or diagonal-ly. By the time we left, the older trees were coming into fruit, hence my concern and questions in my first letter home. Blanche had carried apples in her knapsack to give to our hosts in U.S.A. so she was extremely upset when they had rotted by the time we got there.

Like the Vineries I had had lots of trips to Dodovens. There was one draw-back about this and that was the risk of a confrontation with the geese who lived there. They can be quite aggressive and it was only some years later I learnt that you really can say "Boo" to a goose for it to leave you alone. The best part about the geese were the lovely fluffy yellow goslings they produced.

When not off on other activities we enjoyed playing in the large garden, often with two boys who lived beside the lane at the back of the house. A feature of our play with Michael and David was the fun we had on go-carts down the hill of this lane. These had been built by Father from wooden packing cases and old pram wheels. Or else we built camps and tree houses in the trees and hedges of the garden.

Foremost in the life of my parents was their membership of the Society of Friends, a Society established in the 17th century by George Fox. Fox did not consider it necessary to have special buildings or ordained ministers and the rituals that went with church worship in order to follow Christ's teaching and hear the voice of God.

The faith of Friends rests on their belief that there is a divine spark or 'that of God' in each and everyone of us, also known as the 'Inner Light'. They consider God can speak to all men and women equally consequently denying the need for the authority of ordained clergy to intervene in their endeavours to follow the teaching of Jesus.

Everyone is considered able to take responsibility for their own spiritual enquiries within the worship and comradeship of the Meeting.

The meetings are held in silence except when one of the group feels they can contribute a message that will help people come to a better understanding of each other and the will of God. Leadership is under the direction of a group of elders who quietly guide the meeting as required.

We always went to the religious Meeting held on Sundays at Swarthmore in Plymouth. This was a plain room with no religious adornment just perhaps a vase of flowers placed on a central table. It was light and airy and I remember watching the sun move across the floor as I sat silently. As a child I was not expected to sit through an hour of silent meeting but only join it for the last fifteen minutes after Sunday School for the previous three-quarters of an hour. That short period could seem very long for a lively child who found sitting still a trial. The seats were hard benches with backs, set in a semicircle facing the elders who would sit facing the group and shake hands at the end to bring the Meeting to a close.

CENTERING DOWN IN QUAKER MEETING
The whirling thoughts buzz through the silence –
The troubled mind darts down blind alleys,
Looking in vain for a clear way through
Guilt wells up as thought seeks excuse -
Pride must be quelled to admit fault
The family problems crowd out personal peace.
But silence can heal and at last we are calm
Open to guidance and our need for each other.
Into the peace comes the world of the spirit.
The ending is healing and strength to go on.

Phyllis Gibson, June 1993

Quakers are renowned for their 'social conscience' and my parents were no exception, hence their contribution in helping the refugees. The house was often full of people before we came away (Florrie was

Joan Lawson   Francis Lawson

The family: Blanche, Father, John, Mother, and Louise

no longer living in). These were the refugees from Europe fleeing the terror of the Nazi regime staying in Tobo until a job and home could be found for them. Not all of them could work for my father. I remember being taught to count in Hungarian and on another occasion receiving a beautiful wooden Slovak doll all dressed in national costume by these people who all had tales to tell of how they had managed to get to England. Because of my youth these were not discussed "in front of the children".

Now here Blanche and I were refugees ourselves but on the other side of the Atlantic Ocean and this familiar home was left behind a long way away. I began to wonder yet again what my new home would be like. Would I like Mr and Mrs Linton?

CHAPTER SIX

Arrival in Philadelphia

AFTER ONE NIGHT in Montreal we continued on our travels by train to New York, stopping there for five nights for administration and quarantine purposes and then on to Philadelphia. Of the stay in New York I can remember nothing and Blanche says the same, it was time in limbo, between two worlds. The arrival in Philadelphia is more memorable and there are newspaper pictures from

"In Plymouth, England, both the parents of Blanche Lawson, 10, and Louise, 8, were once active in helping refugees from Germany, Austria, Czechoslovakia. Last night, in New York, Blanche and Louise were themselves refugees." (New York News)

Arrival in Philadelphia (Philadelphia Evening Bulletin)

the *Philadelphia Evening Bulletin* to remind us of the event. One of two solemn little girls still in their pale berets and new summer coats standing worried and forlorn beside their knapsacks and luggage waiting to see who was going to collect them. (see frontispiece) Another shows a picture of the eight Quaker children all waving. There were reporters all round jostling to take our pictures.

"Come on," they called, "look at the camera. That's it. Now how about a wave?"

"Why do they want us to wave?" I asked Blanche. "We're coming; not going. We've only just arrived," I complained.

"What was it like in England when you left? What were the air raids like?" We were asked. Blanche spoke for the two of us.

"Our air raid shelter was cold and I didn't like the spiders," she told them.

"After a while the air raids were rather boring and all that happened was that you were kept awake by having to rush down to the shelter when the siren went and then going back to bed in the house when the 'All Clear' went."

"Why did they call me Joan? My name's Louise," I asked later when I saw what had been written in the paper.

"Well you are Joan Louise quite often at home," Blanche reminded me. "Just like Princess Margaret Rose who is called by two names as well."

There was quite a melee on the station with all us children, our prospective "adopters" and the reporters all milling about. Out of the sea of faces we were finally put with a family called Wood who assured us they were going to look after us and not the Lintons as we expected. Certainly we were in no position to doubt the machinations of the powers that be. Here began what proved to be five very happy years.

Four Woods, Mr. and Mrs. Wood, Rebecca and Anne, had come to meet us and give us a really friendly welcome. After all, this was as momentous an occasion for them as it was for us, taking on these two unknown little girls. They all seemed quite tall: Mr. Wood was the tallest, six feet, with round glasses and hair just beginning to recede, Mrs. Wood was also tall with a centre parting and hair tied back in a bun at the back but much less severe than my Mother's because it was quite wavy so gave a gentler look, Rebecca was nearly as tall as her father with striking red hair, and Anne, who was younger had fair hair. Richard the youngest, who we met later in Moorestown. was also fair.

Six of us climbed into what seemed a very big car. In those days three adults could sit on the broad bench seat in the front and the rest in the back. As the smallest in size, I was to discover that I invariably sat on someone's knee when the whole family went together.

On the drive from Philadelphia to Moorestown, where the Woods lived, we were able to establish that Rebecca and Anne were older than Blanche and I was just three months older than Richard. The journey which meant crossing the Delaware River on a big suspension bridge to the state of New Jersey, was full of talk and new sights. Everyone was at pains to make us feel at home. There were enquiries about our journey and the family left behind, as well as descriptions of what we were to find at Moorestown. We were told that Anne's bedroom had been converted for Blanche and myself while she had graduated to a room of her own on the second floor next to the attics. Fortunately for us, she considered that to have her own eyrie at the top of the house was a good move so she did not feel we were imposing on her.

This arrangement and preparations for our arrival had been quickly organised as the Woods had had only ten days notice that they were to have some evacuees due to the last minute changes of plan. They had been on holiday on the New Jersey shore when they learnt they were to receive two young girls and had hurried home to get ready for our arrival. The Lintons had decided that we were too young for them.

My parents received confirmation of our arrival when a Western Union Cablegram was received.

"BLANCHE AND LOUISE ARRIVED SAFE AND WELL. THEY ARE VERY WELCOME." signed Richard Wood.

This was dated 30th August 1940. We had got to our destination, at last, seventeen days after we left London.

My first letter home from Moorestown is dated the next day but with no address.

Dear Mummy and Daddy,

I hope the whole family is well. I am writing with my new pen I hope you think it writes alright. On Sunday the 25th we went to bed at 12:30p.m. We have had our photos taken lots of times and are going to send them to you. They all look alful. Is John growing a lot. Why didn't you tell us we were coming to the Woods. The Woods are very much home like. The Amerecains eat quite difrent food. We saw six Icebergs. Moorestown is how you said it was. There were six children out of the Q section they were Peter Cooper, Lilla Rowland, Michael Rutter and Pricsilla Rutter and of corse us two which made six. Mrs. Wood was thrilled to see the Jig Saw Puzzle of Jemima Puddle Duck and our best clothes.

> *When are you going to answer this letter.*
> *With double love Louise*
> *X X X X X X X*

So many things were different from England; the first, most notable, was the food we were given to eat. My experience of food from other parts of the world was very limited. Today, supermarkets have food from all parts of the world readily available in season and out, but at this time the cosmopolitan nature of food in ordinary shops was not yet to be seen. Added to this our recent meals in England had been very limited because of the food rationing.

At one of our first meals with the Woods, Mrs. Wood announced, "We are going to have for supper tonight something I don't think you will have tasted before. You will eat it with your fingers."

I had no idea what this treat could be. It turned out to be corn on the cob.

"Well, what do you think of it Louise?"

"It's lovely stuff." I pronounced in my very English accent. The Americans were as delighted with the English accent as with my happy acceptance of such novel food without any fuss. The fact that we could eat something hot in our fingers dripping with butter without a reprimand about table manners was a truly new experience. The Woods were taken with the "lovely stuff" of my description and it was quoted and referred to many times as it became part of family folk lore.

Accompanying my letter was the first letter from Nancy Wood, who we would come to call Aunt Nancy for the duration of our stay; her husband Richard Wood, who had sent the cable, we would call Uncle Dick. This letter had only her initials at the top, the address will have been on the back of the envelope in the American fashion. In this instance it is dated at the bottom, many later letters could only be dated by the post mark on the envelope.

Dear Joan Lawson,

You will have received Dick's cable and so know that your girls are with us, safe and well except for slight sniffles which they tell me all the children contracted on the voyage. They are all unpacked and sorted out, and are now safely tucked in and I hope asleep. I have rubbed Iodex in behind Blanche's knees and promised to make a valiant attack on any spiders there may be - though I hope there are none. They have discovered some games in the nursery closet and are going to have a very quiet time for the next few days just resting up and playing the games.

The poor lambs have had a terrific time of it - with doctor's check ups and various interviews and reporters dogging their footsteps constantly. They landed in Montreal on Sunday and came direct to New York where they stayed for five days as a sort of quarantine period, as there had been both measles and chicken-pox among the group on the way over.

Today we drove over to the station in Philadelphia and met the train from New York bringing the 8 Friends, six of whom have come to Moorestown. The children assure me you know all about us, because Agnes Stokes had written Lilla's mother about us.. (Agnes Stokes was Aunt Nancy's greatest friend and always referred to by our generation as 'Cousin Agnes', an almost Shakespearian use of the word 'cousin' rather than the English practice of adult friends becoming 'honorary' aunts and uncles. She and Aunt Nancy had worked together to arrange homes for the British Refugees who arrived in Philadelphia.)

However, I think you would really learn more from Arthur Gage who stayed with us here in 1937, for all too short a visit.

Our family consists if Dick, age 43 and myself, age 42 and 3 children; Rebecca, 16 a Senior this coming winter, Anne nearly 14 and Richard Junior, 8. They all go to the Friends School, as will your two as well as Peter Cooper and Lilla Rowland. I think Louise and our Richard will be in the same class but as the schools here are quite different from yours they will probably be given some tests a few days before school begins so that they may be properly placed. Am tremendously impressed with your packing. Thanks so much for the pieces of the new frocks. I shall keep them in good repair. Blanche was thrilled with the new blue print you had put in for her. How you ever got it all done so beautifully, on such short notice, I don't see. We think you are quite wonderful. I was so glad when I found I could have your children. We had thought so much about you all and finally Agnes Stokes and I drew up and sent the cable referred to in "The Friend" as the "Cable from New Jersey"

I had known two girls who had been through rather bad times in the Last War (i.e. World War I) and had it very much in my heart to have Friends know that we would be more than happy to share homes with any children whose parents felt it advisable. What you said in the Meeting for Sufferings, as quoted in 'The Friend' is just what I have felt so strongly and we will do our best to give these little girls of yours the love, security and serenity children of their age need.

Blanche seems to feel the responsibility of Louise very much but I dare say the burden will become lighter when they have settled down and really feel at home. They are both such darlings I do hope they may be really happy with us.

I shall try and write regularly every week to let you know how they are getting along. I dare say letters will come to you irregularly - unless the new air service direct to England becomes dependable. A plane made the trip in 13 hours from New York to London not long ago.

I shall hope to hear from you soon, especially if there are any especial health or diet details I should know. Thank you so much for your trust in us. With regards to you all,

    Sincerely,

        Nancy Morris Wood   *Moorestown, 29.8.40*

The mention of Arthur Gage who was a member of the Plymouth Friends Meeting to which my parents belonged is indicative of the close network that exists within the Society of Friends. There is a long history of links between the New World and the Old stretching as far back as the 17th and 18th centuries when Friends travelled across the Atlantic in both directions quite frequently. Whenever Friends move around the world on their travels they invariably take with them an "Epistle" of greeting from their home meeting to that they are visiting. The hospitality offered often includes overnight accommodation. The links are like those of an extended family. Certainly my parents will have been hosts to other Friends visiting the West Country in England.

The article referred to in "The Friend" comes from the issue dated July 12, 1940 where Joan Lawson is quoted as saying; "Parents who contemplated this step were not doing so from fear of air raids, but were concerned for the spiritual and nervous results of war, and anxious to keep their children from oppression". The Meeting for Sufferings also mentioned is the main executive organisation of the Society of Friends in London so called because in its early days it was literally the place where the sufferings and imprisonment of Friends were reported.

Over the years we were in America quite a number of people were found who were known to both my parents and the Woods. In particular, it turned out that a cousin of my Mother's, Ronald Howe, was married to Caroline, the daughter of Carroll (a man's name) and Anna Brown from Westtown, Pennsylvania, where Carroll taught English at the Friends Westtown School and was a great friend of the Woods, in fact he had taught them there I discovered later.

It was a letter from Anna Brown that helped unravel the reason that Blanche and I had ended up in the Wood household and not with the Lintons'. It was Caroline, their daughter, who had made the arrangements in the first place. When my parents had received the cable from Richard Wood they had assumed he had sent it in some official capacity on behalf of Moorestown Friends so it had taken them a little while to realise what had happened and strangely enough Aunt Nancy made no mention of our change of venue in that first letter.

Anna Brown's letter is as follows.

Westtown
Pennsylvania
Monday, September 23, 1940

Dear Mrs. Lawson,
I feel like calling you 'cousin' because of our Caroline who married your cousin, Ronald Howe. You remember that at your suggestion Caroline wrote us about your 2 girls. She gave their ages older than they are and when I received Caroline's letter we had assumed responsibility for 2 other children and so I went to our very good friend, James Vail, who is devoting himself to the (American Friends) Service Committee, one branch of which is working on homes for English Children. He suggested the Lintons as I cabled Caroline. Their children are grown and away and they wanted older girls, so good friends of theirs and ours, the Woods arranged to take yours. We were away at our camp in the Adirondacks and the Lintons were away when all this happened.

All that introduction is just to try and explain what must have seemed like neglect.

We were at dinner yesterday with the Wood family. If you do not know already, they are lovely people and much better really than the Lintons, fond of the Lintons as we are.

You need have no qualms about your children's foster home. Dick and Nancy are two of the choice persons of this world and Blanche and Louise really seemed (except for their unmistakeable accents) like children of the family. Louise and their Richard being twins. After dinner Louise got into Richard's trousers and shirt so as to climb their favorite tree in comfort; and safety for the pretty print dress she had been wearing. Blanche read in the living room where Rebecca and Anne were, one reading and one doing a picture puzzle which the other two occasionally helped with.

We were sitting in the garden with Dick and Nancy and Blanche came out to play with the two younger ones before we left. Nancy suggested she change into an older dress if she was going to climb which she went to do.

Your children have come through the ordeal of the voyage and the change and loneliness much better than the Russell children, who were quite sick for a while, even with their mother; and the Johnson children with whom they are living caught their colds and so on.

Blanche and Louise certainly looked rosy and relaxed. Nancy says that Blanche has wakened in the night scared but apparently at voyage fears or air raids before leaving home because she was comforted and as soon as she knew where she was and went back to sleep and that comforted Nancy who does want them to be the happy members of the family that they seem to be.

Maybe they have sent you pictures? Rebecca, the oldest daughter has sandy red hair and the clear thin skin that goes with it, on the edge of being fat but not quite there, though she used to be. She is almost a young lady as she will be in college next year. She is quietly capable and has been quite competent to look after young Richard for a couple of years. She is past 16 but seems 18. Anne almost 14 (I think she has a birthday in a few days time) is the better looking one, with fair hair curled at the ends, a slender figure and brown eyes. She will probably ignore the 3 younger ones more than Rebecca, but likes them. She sits, or did when we were there, next to Blanche at one side of the table and Rebecca sits between Louise and Richard. Richard is a little taller than Louise and with Anne's hair color. Those two have an 'American skin', fair but with-

out any color in it, though both Dick (we call the father Dick and the son Richard) and Nancy have some color. Nancy is slender and always looks well dressed, though she does not spend much on her clothes - just can't help having an air. My husband, Carroll, thoroughly enjoys him (so do I) they both like taking opposite sides of a question (either side will do) and thoroughly airing it. He is fond of yours as well as his own children but it is Nancy who does all the practical running of the household. I have never seen her cross, nor disobeyed: she is just that kind of person.

I asked Blanche if she remembered a visit that our Caroline paid you when she and Ronald came to Plymouth on their 'honeymoon' and she said she did but that was all she really remembered because she had been in the garden almost all of the time they were there and that she got stung by a wasp.

We hope to be of service if needed as an emergency reserve, and meantime, be as easy in your mind as you can with your girls so far away. They will be as well off as affectionate and intelligent care can keep them. I shall write again after a while to give an outsiders report. I too have a daughter overseas.

Anna Hartshorn Brown

Anna Brown's description of the family gives you a good idea of each of them. I cannot remember Aunt Nancy having an 'air'. She was not a fancy dresser as she would have called it but usually wore 'shirtwaisters' which had the advantage of generally being in fashion. She wore glasses hiding her twinkling brown eyes; glasses that had a tendency to slip down her nose and typically were frequently pushed up again. Her distinctive sense of humour and relaxed style endeared her to us immediately, on the other hand, I was just a little bit in awe of Uncle Dick. This was partly because I was often not quite sure when to take him seriously and when he was pulling my leg. He was very well read and well versed in Quakerism. As a joint editor of the *The Friend* and secretary of The Friends Peace Committee he was aware of Friends' activities throughout the world. He was definitely an Anglophile.

The description of Rebecca is a little unfair, she was more redhead than sandy nor "on the edge of being fat". Her red hair meant that occasionally Uncle Dick would call her "Carrots" which was not appreciated. She was academically very able and won a scholarship to Bryn Mawr College, which is one of the top U.S. colleges on the other side of Philadelphia. Becca, as she was generally called, definitely had the air of the eldest and could keep us in order quite easily.

Anna also got it wrong in her assessment of Anne as she became very involved with us and was often the instigator of games and activities to keep us occupied. Within the family she was often referred to as "Puddy" dating back to her plumpness as a baby, she was more resigned to this nickname than Becca to her "Carrots".

Richard, the youngest and only boy, was always full of imaginative projects and schemes garnered from the adventure stories he read. When we arrived he was having a cowboys and Indians craze; but there were boat phases, newspaper schemes and endless ideas for original play. He had his hair cut in a crew cut something which children in England would never have had at this time.

CHAPTER SEVEN

272 West Main Street, Moorestown

MOORESTOWN, the small town where I was taken to live, was about twenty miles from Philadelphia in the state of New Jersey. It is on the broad flat sandy plain that runs down the whole east side of the United States from Cape Cod to Florida. The land was very well suited to what the English call market gardening and the Americans, "truck farming", where fruit and vegetables were grown to feed the ever expanding urban population from Boston to Washington. This was an enterprise, though done very differently from that which Blanche and I had experienced at home, at least we understood a little bit.

Moorestown was established by Quakers as a settlement in the 17th century not long after Philadelphia was founded. It was in 1682 that William Penn first reached America and claimed land that had been given to his father, Admiral Penn, by Charles II in lieu of a large debt. Rather than commandeer this land from the Indians William Penn, who had become a Quaker, made payment to them and signed a treaty with them thereby ensuring that there was peace in the new settlement which he called Philadelphia, "The City of Brotherly Love", in the state of Pennsylvania.

Quakers also obtained land on the east side of the Delaware River where among the settlements established was Moorestown. The first Quaker Meeting House there was built in 1700; prior to that Friends would worship in their own homes. The Quaker influence was still strong sixty years ago and also today. Even now it is a "dry" town where no alcohol can be bought or sold in keeping with the long held view of Friends that drink can have an evil influence on peoples lives especially when taken to excess.

The Woods lived on West Main Street but for all the town-like address it was a very pleasant area with open lawns, many trees and old clapboard houses, frequently with porches. The houses stood back from the road with no dividing hedges in the front and not many in the back.

My sister and I soon settled in as this next letter from Aunt Nancy verifies.

Mrs. Richard Reeve Wood
272 West Main Street
Moorestown, New Jersey

5.9.1940
Dear Joan Lawson,
Your little girls seem as well and happy as can be. To me they seem almost a miracle they have fitted in to our scheme of life so easily. There have been no tears at all, not once, and the house is full of laughter all day long - as a house should be with children in it. They are helpful and natural; and though I can see that Blanche is high strung - she has not seemed at all on edge. I hope soon she will let me take more responsibility for Louise, and so relieve her of it, but that will naturally develop and I am not pressing her at all.

The letter you sent to Margaret Linton and that you sent to the caretaker on the ship verify me in my own understanding of the children and I think we may look forward to a happy winter. They tell me I am much like you, though perhaps more still like Aunty Helen. (My Aunty Helen was my mother's oldest sister and I am amazed how right we were to compare Aunt Nancy to her. They were both very maternal, very practical, unflappable people; the sort that people turn to in a crisis while my mother on the other hand was more highly strung, a characteristic that it would appear, to have been handed down to Blanche). *Dick is like your husband sometimes laughing and joking at meals until it is "past a joke"; and liking to wear his fearful* ragged old clothes when he has perfectly good one to wear. I could not have asked for sweeter natured more adaptable members of the family. We all love them and they say they feel as though they have been at home with us for a long time.

Although our house is on Main Street of the town, the garden runs back to the open fields with some uncared for apple orchards and Louise and our 8 year old Richard climb there by the hour. I have gotten her 2 regulation gym suits of dark blue, rather lightweight cotton cloth, with v neck and no sleeves and bloomers, all one piece. In the warm weather she wears them without a blouse and they keep her well covered and save her better clothes. Today they went with my big girls to lunch with a friend of Becca's. They cooked their own lunch and played with pony colts and climbed trees and seemed to have a good time.

Tomorrow we may go to arrange about the details at the school but we'll wait to decide until morning as they looked pretty tired at supper time and I am trying not to let them do too much. They are eating magnificently, everything that comes and so far it has agreed with them. I can't thank you enough for having trained them that way, as mine are the same. This summer we had a little niece with us who was very fussy and it is hard on the whole group. Your lambs try everything and generally say "lovely stuff".

My stout middle-aged colored maid, who comes at 2:30 5 days a week enjoys them exceedingly. We give them, the three younger ones, early supper so that they may get to bed in good time and it is working out well. We tried them dining with us but Dick can't be home early and 7 o'clock dinner made them get to bed far too late as there are so many last minute things to be done.

Blanche has had no recurrence of the rheumatism, since the first night they came, though I feel there is some stored up exhaustion which will gradually work away. I judge it to be more spiritual than physical, and I feel it less every day. They take great pleasure in making paper dolls with Anne, sitting about a big tree in the garden, with paints, crayons, scissors and glue all very busy. This afternoon I found them reading fairy tales out loud. Each day they lie down after lunch at 1:30 until 3 or 3:30 if lunch is late; in separate rooms so as to be really quiet.

Yesterday Richard Jr. was offered a tiny grey kitten with 4 white feet and a white front. He brought it at once to see if they wanted it, of course they did, and it is now tenderly cared for by both of them but especially Louise. Blanche gave it a great dose of flea powder at once so I think it will be fairly clean.

I am so thankful that your girls are as unconscious of modesty as all our children, especially Richard, who has grown up entirely naturally with his two sisters as yours have with John. I nearly split this morning when I heard the door open from his room to theirs and looking in found him without a stitch on but his great grandfather's top hat and the kitten on his arm informing them solemnly that he thought they might like to play with it before they got up so he had run down to get it for them. It sleeps in a box in the kitchen.

They have a very light room which we added to the house when Anne was born. It is 16 by 20ft. square with 7 windows. The walls are a peachy tan, the curtains rather the same. The rug is an old fashioned mixed rag one. The beds have new rust colored covers gotten today and new window shades are expected any moment, which will be a relief to Blanche. The house is old, about 1760, with steps up and down. Red brick with quite a lot of old box. We will take some pictures soon and send them when we can.

I am so glad to know your connection with Ronald Howe as Caroline's parents are among our close friends. Dick wrote Arthur Gage a long effusion today. Please give him our warm regards when you see him.

I fear Blanche's note is on the brief side. She is very proud of having decided that it could do as a letter to 6 or 8 people as she feels far too busy to write. I should like her to try a line today but so far she doesn't see that.

with warm appreciation,
Nancy Morris Wood

P.S. I am sorry about the Linton mix up in names. No one quite knows how you got their names. They are darling people but 10 years older than we are and their family all grown and flown and a 4 year old granddaughter. Albert travels a great deal and Margaret goes with him, leaving only maids at home and though they are more well-to-do we thought the

*children would be happier here with other children and older children
would be there.*

Aunt Nancy's use of the word gotten reminds me of all the new
words we were introduced to as we settled into our American home.
Anne would say, "Will thee go get those games from the closet Louise."
"The what?" I would ask. "The closet is what thee calls a cupboard",
she would explain. There were a great many words that were different
or used differently from the English I knew. Words like a faucet for tap,
sidewalk for pavement, erasers for rubbers and galoshes were rubbers;
rubber overshoes to keep your shoes dry in wet weather. Wellington
boots hadn't appeared to have crossed the Atlantic, though they were
regular wear in wet Devon. Tea time became supper time; there was no
such thing as a meal called tea. Puddy's bedroom wasn't on the second
floor but the third storey because the ground floor is counted as
number one and so it went on.

Another fascinating word used by Aunt Nancy was "jitney" for a
hire car. Later I looked up this word to find out about it. It seems it
had come from the French word jeton for a token and it refers to the
jeton or token people would use to pay the driver of the cab dating
back to times when the 'cab' would have been horse drawn. I am not
sure now how many Americans actually use this word or whether it
was an "Aunt Nancyism". She had her own way with words at times as
her use of the word "effusion" to describe Uncle Dick's letter to Arthur
Gage suggests.

The use of "thee" and "thou" within the Wood family was new to us
too, a practice common among Quakers in the past but no longer used
by English Friends. Quakers believed that all men and women were
equal before God and used the terms thee and thou as these were generally used for friends (with a small f) and equals rather than the more
formal you. This belief that all men were equal before God is illustrated
by the well known story of their founder George Fox who would not
raise his hat to the King of England and suffered the consequences.
This "Plain" language was still being used in Moorestown, though
dying out. It tended to be used like the French 'tu' by those nearest to

272. The Wood's family home on the left

you. It is interesting that Aunt Nancy never addressed my mother in her letters using thee or thou.

Reading Aunt Nancy's use of the word gotten brings back to me the trouble I got into when writing my first English essay back in an English School just after returning from America. I was severely reprimanded for using gotten and had to write out lines with the correct use of the word to get. I was quite unaware of my misdemeanour because it was common usage in the United States, nor was it considered bad English. I am still a little surprised that the English teacher was so lacking in understanding. My progress in English never quite recovered and my views on that particular lady hampered me considerably.

The house we lived in with the Woods in West Main Street, usually referred to as Two Seven Two, at 240 years old was remarkably old by American standards. It was what the English call semi-detached, the Woods half being red brick and the next door half being white clapboard was lived in by the Leconeys' and later by a family called Perkins who had a daughter, Patsy, who became one of Blanche's bosom pals.

As mentioned, it stood well back from the road and was approached by a red brick path with the 'old' box hedges on either side. In fact the box had grown across the path to such an extent that it was very difficult to walk up the path between them to the front door, so everyone would walk across the lawn beside it. To this day the characteristic smell of box brings back instant memories of Two Seven Two. The family usually never went to the front door but would enter through the porch under Blanche and my bedroom or further around that porch to the back door.

What interested me about the house was the way you had to go through one room to get to another room, all interconnecting. There were two staircases to get to the first floor, one in the front hall which took you up to the upstairs front landing and another going from the dining room to an upstairs back landing. These two staircases to the first floor gave great scope for games of hide and seek. By going up one staircase and down the other, you could soon escape a pursuer but because the floors were bare boards with occasional mats it meant the rushing about of the 'Young' created a lot of clatter. "Come on children, go and play outdoors," we would be told.

Emma, the stout middle-aged "colored" maid was an important part of the household. Blanche and I were familiar with having domestic help in the house but this was our first close encounter with a black person and we soon came to appreciate her good humour and home cooking. Besides helping with the cooking Emma also helped with the washing and the ironing which was a considerable chore in a household of seven which including dresses for four girls.

These were the days when the washing at Tobo, back in England, was boiled in a big copper kettle in the corner of the wash house, an extra lean-to at the back of the kitchen. The whole wash house filled with hot foggy steam as the copper boiled. Once boiled the heavy towels and sheets could be pulled out with tongs to be rinsed in two deep stone sinks with a hand mangle between them, so the whites could be rinsed on one side, put through the wringer to the other side for the second rinse and back again. All heavy back breaking work and Blanche and I knew better than to get in the way of this demanding task on a Monday morning. Rain or shine it was always on a Monday.

By contrast the washing at *272* was done in an electric washing machine with an electric mangle, quite a new fangled labour saving devise. Not quite as labour saving as those we have today; a top loader with paddles that swished back and forth in the suds, it still needed standing over to be filled with water with hoses and emptied again then the clothes put through the electric mangle. However, a lot of the backache was removed.

The drying was different too. In Moorestown it was clothes line with a prop, and woe betide the person who knocked the pole down when rushing about the back yard and put the clean washing on the ground.

At Tobo the clothes lines were hung between two very tall poles so there was a top line and a bottom line. The top line was pulled up and down by a system of ropes and pulleys a method developed by the people of Plymouth with a long seafaring tradition and a familiarity with ships and their rigging.

CHAPTER EIGHT

School and adjustment

T HE NEXT BIG EVENT was starting school. We were to go to the Moorestown Friends School with the rest of the family. First Blanche and I were given tests to decide which class we should be put in. It was quickly decided that I should join Richard in his class but there was more concern about Blanche as she had studied different subjects and to different levels in our English School compared to this new American School as this letter from Blanche explains.

c/o Mrs. Wood
272 West Main Street
Moorestown
New Jersey, U.S.A.
26th Sept 1940

Dear Mummy and daddy,
We have just started school and the name of are teacher is Miss Swan, they say that she is one of the best teachers in the school. She is really afully nice. I am in the sixth grade and Louise is in the fourth grade and they don't have French, Latin or Algebra and I am very sad about it.
*   When am I going to get your next letter. We have only had two letters since we have been hear. I don't think there is much more to tell you.*
Love from
*   Blanche*

Both these classes were in the Elementary School of Moorestown

Moorestown Friends School

Friends School; Blanche in the sixth grade would have been in the top elementary class and the following year she would go up to Junior High School which included seventh and eighth grade. After that it was High School where Anne and Becca were.

The School we had attended in England, called Rocky Hill Preparatory School, and run by a Mr. Richardson, was in Plymstock, a suburb of Plymouth, which we reached by bus each day from our home in Elburton. It had unimaginative teaching and a lady teacher who would smack your open palm with a ruler if work or behaviour was not to the required standard. This teacher had a spinsterish look, though she may well have been married for all I knew, with steel rimmed glasses, hair pulled back in a bun who wore cardigans similar to Miss Andrews. Our American teachers, with the exception of Miss Swan, were all a lot younger and a little more dressy. I invariably had a crush on my young games teacher all through my American School days.

At Rocky Hill we wore a grey uniform and that included those awful bowl shaped felt hats beloved by English schools at that time, replaced by equally bowl shaped panamas in the summer. What a joy to have no uniform or corporal punishment at our new school.

Miss Swan was not young but was described by Aunt Nancy as having a quiet manner that gave the children confidence as well as getting the best from them. She was never satisfied with less than the best but if the best is not perfect she would be helpful and kind. Anne encouraged Blanche "Thee'll love Miss Swan, Blanche, she is our best teacher, and both Becca and I loved being in her class."

A school routine was soon established in the mornings. Helped by Anne, Aunt Nancy provided each of us with a coloured lunch box with two sandwiches and a matching thermos full of milk, mine was red Richard and Blanche both had green. Besides that we each got 10 cents to buy soup or a sweet or, if you could wait, an ice cream bought at the drug store on the way home. We would leave the house at "quarter after" eight (not quarter past) to go the three-quarters of a mile along Main Street to get to the school at the other end. Blanche and Anne rode bikes while Becca, Richard and I walked. Later we would go on bikes as well.

I well remember the sidewalk separated from the roadway by a small strip of grass and trees. It was a pretty path made of red bricks laid in a pattern, not always even because the growing tree roots would lift it in places. In autumn the path would be covered in fallen leaves which we would kick through scattering their crackling pretty colours before us. The leaf colours in autumn could be breathtaking reds and yellows with all shades in between. The sugar maples and dogwoods were the most spectacular.

One of the chores at school was having to learn by heart long pieces from the Scriptures such as the 121st Psalm. Blanche particularly hated doing this and all of us did it reluctantly. Other than that we all enjoyed our time at school immensely. Blanche enjoyed it even though she found the work difficult. Aunt Nancy constantly worried about it and many times in letters she voiced her concern. Blanche had done some quite difficult work at Rocky Hill but it would seem some of the basics to the understanding of it still eluded her. Aunt Nancy's daughters were always at the top of their classes so finding Blanche struggling was unfamiliar.

Soon after we started I came home one day and announced;

"I've been put on the Flower Committee." I was delighted with this new responsibility.

Richard replied, "Gee, well, I'm on the Bird Committee; I don't think I'll have to do much."

"Well, I'm going to make a collection of wildflowers." I replied.

I took my new task very seriously. I had been provided with a lovely new red scrap-book and a piece of sea lavender to press and put in it to start me off. I set off enthusiastically into the meadow behind the house looking for further specimens. Here the golden rod and purple asters, not to mention the blackberry thickets, were well above my head but I carried on like an African explorer into the jungle, all in the interests of science. I returned with some good specimens which were identified in the family flower book and pressed in heavy tomes to be put in the lovely new book.

Unfortunately, I returned not with just flowers but a terrible rash from poison ivy. I had not known about poison ivy before but I certainly learned about it now. In England we had stinging nettles which, though painful, were usually assuaged with spit on a dock leaf placed on the afflicted area. The sting would go fairly soon to be replaced by a tingling then itching sensation that generally did not last more than an hour or so. Not so with poison ivy. I had at least three days off school. Blanche looked at me rather alarmed and said, "Do you know, Louise, your face is all swollen, one eye is shut and you have red patches all over your legs."

I knew all right because it hurt and itched all at the same time. Doctor Emlen Stokes, the local doctor and family friend, was duly consulted and a long warm bath with cornstarch dissolved in it was prescribed followed by a wipe all over with cotton wool dipped in a curing Calamine Lotion. Lying for a long time in the bath was a rare luxury. It was a week or two before Aunt Nancy reported it had all cleared up.

Luckily, this did not entirely dampen my enthusiasm for flowers because the next we learn is about my efforts at growing them from seed. The fact that this was at the wrong time of year for seed growth followed by an excessive amount of watering meant a sad end for this particular scientific venture.

For me the most exciting pursuit at our American School was the chance to learn and play hockey after school. Blanche and I both really enjoyed this and it was the beginning of successful hockey careers for both of us. We both played for our school, our University and our County. My greatest achievement was to play for the English Universities eleven in International matches, all springing from the skill and eagerness of the athletic teachers at Moorestown Friends School. As my rather scrappy letter of 4th October 1940 tells my parents.

> *Dear Mummy and Daddy,*
> *This afternoon I and Richard had are first violin lessons and I am going to have a new book.* (More about the violin lessons later*). At school we have hoky and I am quite good at it. Blanche has put on 9 pounds. Richard's birthday is on March the 30th, Rebecca's is June 26th, Anne's is September 30th. I have made a rag doll and making clothes for it.*
> > *Unsigned.*

As I shall tell birthdays were special events for the whole family.

The ease with which we adapted into our American family was really quite remarkable. Apparently we talked of England and everyone left behind frequently and yet were content to become part of our new family with no qualms. My school report at the end of that first term comments "One has not been conscious that Louise has had to make any effort to adjust. The children appreciate her ability and she is very much one of the group. She is courteous and cooperative in her relationships, while continuing to maintain her individuality. Does not always plan her time wisely. She is a very welcome addition to the group". In case I should appear as too much of a paragon here, I should add that it was politely noted that arithmetic and history were not my favourite subjects and there was a tendency to be in too much of a rush and not spend enough time on my work on occasion.

Similarly, in a letter I wrote at about the same time I say: *I am sorry I haven't been writing to you. We have been having such a good time I can hardly tell it all, but I will tell you as much as I can.* There follows a list of all the things I am giving and making everyone for Christmas.

There is no doubt that our common Quaker background and stan-

Moorestown Quaker Meeting House

dards had much to do with how we settled into our American family. The atmosphere at 272 must have had a familiarity about it that was in no way alarming to us. Going to Quaker Meeting every Sunday had been very much a feature of our lives in England and so it was in Moorestown as well. The main difference was that now we were expected to sit through a whole hour of meeting preceded by an hour of Sunday School. The experience of silently sitting still through an hour long meeting was a lot more demanding than the 15 minutes in England.

I was old enough to understand the basic principles of the religion practised by my parents and the Wood family and learnt to appreciate the opportunity for silent reflection as I grew older. However, this did mean I found sitting through an hour of predominantly silent Meeting quite a taxing exercise especially when there was ministry by a member I might find rather tedious because of the adult nature of the discourse. Not only did we have to stay quiet we also had to keep still with no fidgeting as even that could interrupt the depth of silence that could develop within a successful hour of worship. Hushed 'sshing' would be aimed at Richard and me if we made too much noise. We would try to make our thoughts concentrate on "higher" matters but it could be more entertaining to peer around to see if any of our elders and betters had gone to sleep.

CHAPTER NINE

Cowboys and Indians

AFTER MY ARRIVAL RICHARD and I became inseparable playmates endlessly inventing projects and activities to keep ourselves occupied. Aunt Nancy was pleased about this as she considered his playmates at the time to be of "meagre" background. Those playmates who lived nearby were handy companions so the reason for her saying this may have been because one of them went to Public School rather than the Friends School but more likely the word "meagre" could be taken literally. However, as I remember it, this did not bother me at all and I just joined the group much of the time. Richard's imagination was never at a loss for a game idea.

When I arrived the current phase was cowboys and Indians, skilfully encouraged by two radio programmes which provided role models. These were "Tom Mix, the Cowboy" and "The Lone Ranger" with his palomino horse, Silver, and his faithful companion Tonto, which were broadcast around five o'clock every weekday afternoon.

"Lou," Richard would say, "Go in and see what the time is." In I would go, breaking off whatever I was doing, hoping no one would see if my shoes made muddy marks on the floor and report back. "It's five of five," I would call out. "Hurry up or we'll miss the beginning."

Whatever was happening then, had to stop so we could rush indoors and huddle around the radio set in time to hear those first stirring bars of the William Tell Overture that introduced the programme accompanied by the theme words "The Lone Ranger rides again; High Ho, Silver, Away!" The stories centred on cattle rustling, stampedes, Indian raids and barbed wire fences with a very clear story line to distinguish the "goodies" from the "baddies". The story always ended on a note of high suspense that would ensure we listened again the next day. Who amongst us and our friends would have to play the "Baddy" and who the "Goody" was always a matter of hot debate because we all wanted to act the hero.

My letter describing these activities is as follows.

Sept 13 1940

Dear Mummy and Daddy,
I (hope) you are well. I am learning a lot about cowboys and Indians from Richard Wood. This afternoon I am going to play a Rodeo. We have two tents in the garden.

When I want to be a cowboy I put on Richard's long trousers and a jersey and a hanky round my neck. The two big girls say I look cute. I was the person to climb the big coffee tree in the (garden) *and they were afraid I would fall.*

On Wednesday we started school and it (is) *lovely.* (I'm) *in Grade 4; their is a little English girl from Saulkum* (Salcombe near Kingsbridge, Devon) *called Macdonald do you know them. I must go to bed.*

Louise
XXXXXXXXXXXXXXXXXXXXXXXXXXXXXXXXXXXXXXXXXX

This was obviously written in a great hurry to get it done before the rodeo and still only just got done before bedtime.

At the rodeo, Richard was initiating me into the difficult task of lassooing calves.

"Look, Lou, thee has to swing the rope around and around in a circle over thy head and then throw it. Look, like this."

"But it gets all tangled up." I would reply as I practiced on a post in the ground again and again.

"It would be more fun if we had some real calves." I suggested to Richard. Real calves were out of the question but Richard pressed Woozer, the family black cocker spaniel into action as a substitute calf. She was not always cooperative in this role, especially when it meant having her legs swept from under her so she could be held to the

Louise in cowboy clothes with Blanche on right

ground and branded. Fortunately, she was very good tempered and her response to our attentions was merely to escape at the first opportunity.

The tents in the garden were instead of Indian tepees. Being an Indian required skill with bows and arrows so a lot of time was devoted to making the bows and the arrows and fitting feathers on the arrows to make them authentic. Wishfully we contemplated shooting a bird to improve our choice of feathers.

In February 1941 there is evidence that our fascination with cowboys and Indians was continuing. At this time Blanche and I were visited by a reporter from one of the Philadelphia papers to see how we were faring in our American home. It included a picture of me in my cowboy clothes in which I look anything but cute. They were an extremely scruffy pair of Richard's trousers. You need to remember that this was before the days when jeans became common wear and little girls were supposed to wear dresses not trousers. Richard is seen in his much treasured wild west ten gallon stetson cowboy hat. The article tells of our latest venture under the headline "Refugees talk American":

Take the home of Mr. and Mrs. Richard Wood, 272 W. Main St., Moorestown as a typical example of the English Refugees. Here Blanche and Joan Louise Lawson, lately of bomb-blasted Plymouth, the English coastal town, play with young Richard Wood. Blanche is 11, two years older than both her sister and her foster brother.

The Editorial Team, Louise, Richard and Blanche

When visited the three had just finished their afternoon naps and were editing a non-commercial enterprise of their own imagination, The Straight Shooters Press, a one issue magazine "with cover an all".

Their child-written articles were not concerned with imaginary exploits of RAF airmen chasing nasty Nazis. They include such titles as "The Lariat", "Skunk Sullivan", "Kit Carson", "Buffalo Bill", "The Mirage" and "The Care of Horses".

"A mirage is a reflection of the sky on a sandy desert," wrote Joan Louise, whose father grew tomatoes under glass before the bombs began to fall. "A cowboy wishes it is water for his horse and himself. A few clumps of grass, no water except for the water in his canteen. His horse is thirsty too. There is a skeleton and a cactus which is of no use. The cowboy looks sadly at the mirage."

In the *Skunk Sullivan* thriller, (written by Richard) "Skunk is a calf rustler and he has killed some men too. He eludes pursuit and is trailed to the hills. The posse went up to the hill. They found Skunk there, stark dead. He had been pricked by a cactus. He thought he had been bitten by a rattlesnake, and there were rattlesnakes up there, so while he was thinking he was dead a rattlesnake did bite him and that was the end of Skunk."

This piece might have been written by any American boy or girl who listens to the "Crime Does Not Pay" radio program.

I continued an enthusiasm for Indians for a long time. There was real excitement on my tenth birthday when I was given a real archery set.

"Oh, look!" I exclaimed, "Arrows with real sharp metal points".

"Now thee realises, Lou, that thee has to be especially careful how thee uses this bow and those arrows," Uncle Dick advises. "That is why we have given thee a bale of hay to go with it on which to put thy target."

I was expected to take this responsibility seriously which I certainly did. By setting the bale of hay and target at the bottom of the garden anything that missed the target would go into the back field away from danger.

There were a number of ways in which my interest was encouraged. One was a project I did at school on Hiawatha. In the long 'Song of Hiawatha' by Longfellow we learnt pieces by heart and by doing this I learnt the Indian words used in the poem, what they meant and the Indian way of life. I could picture in my mind the life of the Indians living close to and understanding the wilderness in which they lived. I even wrote brother John a letter on birch bark that I had collected on a walk through the woods.

There were many stories known to Friends about their history as early settlers in the 'New Land' that were associated with their relationship with the Native Indians. Frequently we would learn about them in school or Sunday School. When the Quaker settlements were first established in Pennsylvania and New Jersey, they were greatly helped by Penn's Treaty with the Indians. By buying the land they settled on from the Indians rather than taking it in battle, William Penn and the early Quakers were able to live in mutual trust while they were establishing Philadelphia, "The City of Brotherly Love", on the banks of the Delaware River.

These arrangements lasted well for the first seventy years of the

Colony but after that time non-Quakers gained control and hostilities developed between the two groups. Even so, the Quakers still endeavoured, when they could, to remain friendly and continue their trust in the local tribes.

There is a tale of a Quaker family living in a fairly remote area where a band of fierce Indians were hiding and they and their neighbours were very apprehensive. This particular family never shut the door at night because they wished the Indians to be aware that they were their friends. On this occasion they had heard that the Indians were on the warpath and likely to attack.. Their neighbours had locked their doors and put their guns to hand in case of trouble. The Quaker family were equally worried but the father refused to lock his door. The mother was most unhappy to think how much danger they were in and got up in the night to lock the door. However, when she got back to bed she could not sleep so soon went down again to unlock it and the family slept peacefully until morning. They then learned that their neighbours had been attacked, their houses burned and many killed while they had been spared.

Later they discovered what had happened from a friendly Indian. The Indians had planned to attack all the houses and take the guns but one amongst them had exclaimed that there was one family that had no guns nor did they lock their door at night. The attacking Indians decided to test the door before they attacked and lo and behold, it was not locked, nor, when they crept about the house did they find any guns; only the family sleeping peacefully. The family never awoke, the only indication of the visit was a white feather stuck over the door. The family was never threatened again.

Another source of enlightenment on the subject of Indians was Uncle Charlie. Uncle Charlie was married to Richard's Grandfather Wood's sister, Anna, who lived next door to the Wood grandparents at Riverton near the banks of the Delaware River about five miles from Moorestown. Uncle Charlie was a factory executive and in his spare time a keen amateur archaeologist. I would go with him to the sandy area behind his house and we would find real Indian arrowheads lying on the ground.

Louise and Richard in play clothes in 1943

"Were these small sharp pointed stones really used by real Indians?" I asked. I could not believe the Indians had been so close to where I was standing. My imagination was fired at the prospect.

I soon became Uncle Charlie devotee and luckily for me he was happy to become my mentor and take this enthusiastic little girl under his wing. At every opportunity I would spend time with him while he would answer my endless questions.

CHAPTER TEN

Birthdays

B IRTHDAYS IN THE Wood family were always an excuse for
a family celebration. We soon learned that there was not a lot
of money for buying presents so making something ourselves
for whoever's birthday it was, was not only cheaper, but involved a lot
of secret activity before the appointed day which added to the mounting excitement. The first "Wood" birthday we experienced was Anne's
when she would be fourteen. As a treat for Anne, and as it turned out
for all the family as well, there was to be a trip to the cinema.

"I'm really not sure I should take you younger ones to the matinee at
the movies." Aunt Nancy said.

"Oh, please." Blanche and I begged "We've never been to the
cinema. What would we see?" we asked.

"There are five Walt Disney cartoons on," replied Aunt Nancy, "two
'Donald Ducks,' 'The Ugly Duckling,' 'Ferdinand the Bull' and 'Snow
White and the Seven Dwarfs'. I'm not sure that 'Snow White' is quite
suitable because the Wicked Witch is rather scary and I don't want you
all having nightmares."

"Oh, please!" we begged, with Richard joining in.

"I think what we will do," Aunt Nancy decided, "is when the Wicked
Witch appears on the screen you must shut your eyes when I say and
keep them shut till she is gone." We three happily agreed.

Off we went, nine of us with Anne's extra friends, to an exciting
afternoon of Walt Disney. I did hide my eyes but a peak through my
fingers was enough for me to keep them hidden.

Afterwards there was a birthday supper with present opening, ice cream and birthday cake with candles. Not fruit cake this time but angel food cake which was light and spongy and melted in your mouth, a special treat.

Blanche had spent a lot of time making a linen case to hold Anne's sewing silks, carefully cross-stitched with "ANNE" embroidered on the flap typical of the sort of presents we gave each other.

The next birthday would be Blanche's when she would be eleven years old and everyone was anxious that she would not feel homesick when it came. Fortunately, a well timed prettily decorated celebration cable arrived from Plymouth on the morning of the Big Day. A lot of trouble was taken over the birthday supper with a damask tablecloth and the best china to make it a special event. Miss Swan, her teacher, and one of Blanche's school friends came to the supper where all the presents were piled on the table in front of her.

Anne and I had joined forces and made a special little sewing box out of a carefully lined cigar box. My contribution was a new pincushion made by hand to go with all the other sewing notions to fill the new box. Everyone had made a special effort with their presents so Blanche was as happy as could be, especially as her special treat outing was still to come.

This time the rest of us did not get to share the treat, which was a trip to the zoo with Lilla Rowland one of the other evacuees who had come from England with us and was a little older than Blanche. I heard all about it when she got back.

"We saw some chimpanzees who rode tricycles and roller skates, walked on tight-ropes, played on a seesaw, said their prayers and kissed their keeper goodnight."

"What did you like best?" I wanted to know.

"Oh the best bit was when we were allowed into the cage with the baby elephant. Aunt Nancy knew the keeper so we were the only ones allowed in. Then even better we rode bare back on the baby elephant with everyone else watching. We gave the baby elephant an apple as well as the hippo and the big elephant."

"Oh, you were lucky," I said enviously wondering whether I would have such an exciting day when my birthday came.

A poignant letter from Grandpa Lawson to Blanche has survived and it shows how different were the feelings of those left behind in England.

3rd. Oct. 1940

My Dear Blanche,

Gran joins with me in wishing you a very happy day on 23rd of this month and joys and blessings in the new year of your life. Also, many happy returns of THE DAY. I think it will be the first birthday on which we have not seen you, never-the-less, you are frequently in our thoughts and our love for you is greater than ever. We are very glad that you have such a nice new home with those who care so lovingly for you and for Joan Louise.

Now I am sure you wish to know about John. He has just been into my office hiding behind the door and when I have asked "Where is John?" he has jumped out with roars of laughter and then hid again. He is growing a lovely boy.

Your Father has been busy in the Apple Orchards many days lately. We have had a warm summer and the apples are splendid this year. Mother has shown me the pretty needle case which she has made for your birthday, I am sure you will like and value it.

Gran is still very ill but she always smile every time John comes in and takes her hand in his.

We all send you our best love,
Yours, Grandpa

And our grateful thanks to Mr. and Mrs. Wood and our best wishes to them and their three children. It would be a tremendous joy if we could see you all.

The nurse referred to in one of our early letters helped to care for Granny Lawson. My memories of Granny are dim but all the stories in the family about her, painted her as a lovely person with a lively sense of humour which my Father had inherited. I remember she always wore a velvet choker with a clasp around her neck. Grandpa Lawson was a energetic and successful business man. When we were little we would be allowed to climb on his lap and pull his pointed reddish beard.

My birthday, on 5th December, when I was nine is well described in a letter from Blanche dated the 8th December and written by Becca because Blanche was ill in bed.

Dear Mummy and Daddy,
I cannot write as I have a bad headache. I didn't go to meeting so Becca brought me home and told me to go to bed.

   Louise had a very happy birthday like Anne and I had. She got a sled from Aunt Nancy as it was snowing. On her birthday a little girl in her class called Janet Haines came to supper and brought with her some balloons which Lou had great fun trying to burst. She got all her presents at supper except three. Becca gave her a red corduroy hat which she had been asking for. One of Becca's aunts gave her a book called "Heidi Grows Up".

   A long time before Louise's birthday, Georgie, the gardener, washed the dolls house; then he and Aunt Nancy brought it up to our room. We all began to make furniture for it. For Lou's birthday I gave her an iron and washing machine which she thinks is great fun because she can wash real doll's clothes in it. Aunt Nancy and Anne and Grandmother gave her a family (for the doll's house); mother, baby, boy, and girl. Another Aunt of Becca's gave her a cook.

   Louise and I had great fun as it was our first time sledding. To make the track we went down the hill on trays. It was the deepest snow we've ever seen
Lots of love
      Blanche
Per Becca

As my birthday was so near Christmas my treat was a visit to Santa Claus, as we soon learnt to call Father Christmas. Santa Claus was to be found in his grotto at Wanamaker's the big department store in Philadelphia. My friend Mary Joy came with me and we had great fun testing all the big toys like automobiles and slides and "oohed" and "aahed" at all the expensive dolls in the toy department before having supper in the tea room. I well remember the fun we had with the straws we got with our milkshakes. They came wrapped in paper and if you opened the paper at one end you could blow the paper off like a little aeroplane to float away across the room. Fortunately, the waitresses put up with these antics with good grace.

CHAPTER ELEVEN

Politics, elections and war

MY WORLD ONCE settled in America was bounded by my home in Moorestown, school and my friends, Sunday School and Sunday Meeting. These occupied most of my thoughts and activities but I was, even at that age aware of the larger world outside. Young though I was hadn't I recently crossed the Atlantic and been moved half-way across the world from one culture to another because of the state of Europe? I knew why I had been sent to America.

Nevertheless, the war being raged in the world while we were in America seemed quite remote. I was aware that it was going on, and could remember the air raids I had experienced before leaving England, but day-to-day it was easily forgotten. After all, the reason for my being there was so this could be the case. Similarly what was happening in the American news was not always of any particular concern.

However, the event of an American election is hard to avoid if you happen to be living in that country at the time. Thus my first introduction to politics had been early on in my time in America when I witnessed the Presidential Election of 1940. I was not quite nine years old when this election was taking place. Nobody can miss what is going on, nobody can miss the razzmatazz. There were posters and campaign badges everywhere. Then, I enjoyed the colourful badges more than what they stood for.

Later, in 1945, I became more aware of the impact of politics on our lives and enjoyed discussions on the subject, in particular with my father once back home in England.

> *Our exciting election is nearly here. It is the hardest decision I have ever had to make about voting"* (wrote Aunt Nancy in November 1940*). "Both men are excellent: Mr. Wilkie is an experienced businessman, Mr.Roosevelt has had no experience in business and the financial condition in the country is bad. Also our method of unemployment relief has created a large group of people who accept state support as a right and have lost any wish to really work. On the other hand the Roosevelt social reforms have been good, his housing reforms have been good and his foreign policy is good and we think that most important of all. However, we don't like the third term. People who know Wilkie say he is much finer than his speeches. Business has confidence in him, which is greatly needed. We were enthusiastic over his nomination and have been cooling ever since due to his bad speeches; but they may be written by other people and should he be elected he may again stand on his own feet and shake off the conservatives of the Republican Party who are making a good deal of noise at present.*

It would appear that Wilkie's speeches produced the same detrimental feelings in other Americans as well and he lost the election.

Who the Wood family finally voted for on this occasion I do not know. It is likely it was Roosevelt, because the Democrats had more of a social programme than their opponents which I would have expected to be more in sympathy with the Quaker view on helping those less fortunate than yourself. Many of their friends will have voted Republican as the party more akin to business. To some extent this may have been a response to what we English would call their "Middle Class" circumstances. They sent their children to a fee paying private school and Grandfather Wood was the director of a company involved with business. Aunt Nancy's concern for Roosevelt's skills in business reflect this.

Later on in one of Uncle Dick's rare letters to my father, he wryly comments that "even the Republican Party is adopting quite respectable resolutions about sharing in the task of making and keeping a decent peace." This was in contrast to its pre-war isolationist policies and reflected his own strongly held views on war.

Dick and Nancy Wood kept abreast of developments in the war in Europe, not least so they would have some idea of the impact it was having on my own parents at home in Plymouth. Generally they were much more closely involved in the work of Friends than in global politics, especially as Uncle Dick worked for a Friends' organization and Aunt Nancy was on various Friends' Committees at different times.

An example of this is when Aunt Nancy writes about the work of American Friends in Europe who had travelled behind German lines before the U.S.A. joined the war and told of what they saw.

Reports reaching this Committee in March 1941 tells of two American Friends who visited Europe to discover the extent of the suffering there as the war progressed. On this occasion they learned about the situation in England, Spain, Germany, Scandinavia, Switzerland and Unoccupied France. At this time the U.S.A. was not in the War and so as neutrals they were allowed access to these countries though travel was difficult. In Scandinavia they had had freedom to see and talk to whomever they wished. There was particular concern about Belgium, Unoccupied France and Spain where the calorie intake for some was as low as 1100 per day. Spain was badly organized for rationing with the result that 'Starvation walked the streets'.

Not long after this the news came of the attack on Pearl Harbour on 7th December 1941 by the Japanese Air Force. This was an horrific shock to all America. It immediately brought America into the War.

Blanche kept asking, "Do you mean **we** are in the War?" meaning the U.S.A. in this instance.

The answer, of course, was "Yes".

"We'll be rationed, you know," was the reply.

To the Quakers of Moorestown for whom war was totally abhorrent it was a very bitter blow. For Uncle Dick who spent a great deal of his time preaching peace and reconciliation it was enough to make him feel quite ill and he went about in a sort of dazed condition after he had heard the news. He considered participating in the killing of other human beings a quite dreadful act. It was a matter he felt very strongly about. On the occasion of this war he signed on for fire duty though beyond his training I do not believe he became actively involved in putting out fires. He found the training interesting because it brought him into contact with very different people than he normally met. My father back in Plymouth was also a fire fighter but he was much more actively involved as I shall tell.

One of the first responses to the war was the setting up by Friends of a local Peace Committee to find ways of being of service to the Community beyond the ways already planned by the local boards. There was a need for extra help in hospitals and social agencies to stand in for others gone to the War. Becca became involved in auxiliary nursing and Uncle Dick helped in a mortuary.

By October 1941 laws on conscription had been passed in the United States. The Quakers with their strong pacifist beliefs were very involved in making arrangements for young men who might make a stand against participating in military service. Aunt Nancy reports on a Representative Meeting she attended when the conscription question was discussed.

Representative Meeting was an administrative meeting for dealing with organisational matters concerning a number of individual Religious Meetings within a region. As Friends have no clergymen to do the administration, it relies on all members of the Society participating in these affairs. On this occasion the traditional Pacifist Groups within the United States were being allowed to set up suitable camps where conscientious objectors could, under pacifist auspices, do work other than military, contributing to the National welfare. This work was generally forestry and forest fire fighting.

At this particular Representative Meeting the impact of conscription was discussed at length. Quakers and other pacifist churches would be expected to pay their own young men, about $35.00 per man per month while they were doing these non-combatant jobs. However, a large percentage of the people registering as conscientious objectors had no religious affiliation. Who would support them while they were in alternative employment? In the circumstance it was decided that Friends would pay for these as well because by so doing the control of

Memorial Day Parade

the camps would stay in their hands, even though it would mean considerable expense to the Society.

As the war progressed, rationing was introduced first for petrol and sugar then later butter and other food items. The only clothing to be rationed was shoes; this was not a problem, especially for me, as at every opportunity I would go barefoot. Because we were a large family the food rationing was not too great a hardship either and it had the advantage that the supply was guaranteed whereas those items in short supply and unrationed could disappear from the shelves of the local store causing inconvenience to all.

I well remember the alternative to butter, called Oleo Margarine. It arrived as an unappetising lump of white fatty substance into which we had to mix the little packet of orange dye to make it have a closer resemblance to the butter it was replacing though the taste was hardly in competition with butter.

The "'gas" rationing caused inconvenience as well. By May 1942 the ration was 3 gallons a week but it needs to be remembered that the cars would only go fifteen miles to the gallon. At the Memorial Day Parade in the summer of 1942 Blanche, her friend Patsy Perkins from next door and I used this theme when we rode in Patsy's pony cart with the notice: "WE NEED NO GAS, NO TYRES JUST A LITTLE SUGAR."

With the War now becoming closer to our side of the Atlantic we decided we should do something to help the "War Effort".

"What shall we do?" we asked ourselves as I was playing with Blanche and Patsy one day. Patsy, who was Blanche's age, often took the lead in our play.

"I think we girls should collect waste paper," Patsy suggested.

"What are you going to do, Richard?" we asked. "You boys ought to do something, the same as us."

"Oh, gee I don't know." he replied. "We'll come up with an idea, don't worry." So Richard went into conference with his pal Charlie Robinson from down the road.

"We've decided to collect scrap metal." they announced.

So we set to action at our allotted tasks. A necessary piece of equipment was a wagon to pull our acquisitions home after visiting all the long suffering neighbours for contributions. We girls proved quite successful collecting paper, whereas the boys found it a little harder to persuade people to part with their old saucepans.

In the summer of 1943 when Mussolini fell there was a feeling that the end of the war was coming and there is the first talk of our return. In fact it would be another two years before that was to happen. It was soon after this that Michael and Priscilla Rutter went home. They had been in the same group as us travelling to America and had gone to different families even though they were both younger than I was. Priscilla had been five when she left home and the whole experience had been unhappy for her. They returned via Portugal that was a neutral country in the conflict.

The end of hostilities was still a long way away and its impact was continuing to be felt. When Anne graduated from school in the summer of 1944 nearly half the boys in her class were absent as they had already left for training. Then in the following Fall Blanche heard that her friend from Elburton, Michael Cummins, was joining the services. This was several months before his seventeenth birthday. Michael and his younger brother David had been our playmates at home in

England. Was Michael really going to become part of this awful War? That brought the European War close to us once more.

Some World events stand out. Of all the historical events that occurred during my stay in America the death of Franklin Roosevelt was the most dramatic. I came home from school that day, 12th April 1945, to find Emma our maid in tears. Emma was a hard working patient soul who put up with my rushing in and out of her kitchen with good grace and humour and to find her with tears streaming down her face was quite alarming. She told me the news. He was the politician who had brought in the New Deal which helped to get the country out of the Depression. The Depression was still a raw memory with many Americans even in the early forties. Following the Stock-market crash on Wall Street in 1929 businesses had crumbled and by 1932 there were 15 million Americans out of work. Emma and her family had only survived this time by keeping pigs and hens and becoming self-sufficient. They knew that F.D.R. had helped more poor people than any President before him and admired him greatly for this. His going was felt like a personal loss. Roosevelt was a Democrat and was into his fourth term of office when he died.

CHAPTER TWELVE

Christmas 1940

TWO CHRISTMASES STAND out in my childhood as particularly memorable; the first one I had in America and the first one I had back in England when I came home in 1945. In both instances a special effort was made to make them memorable after the changes I had experienced in the previous months. The first one I had with the Woods is well described in the letter Aunt Nancy wrote to my Mother on 26th December 1940, the day we call Boxing Day in England but which has no great significance in the United States

Dear Joan,
Thank goodness for your letter of the 5th which came in Lou's pyjamas. (Note the Lou; by now I was always called Lou. It was only many years later when teaching in a boys school that I reverted to Louise because I felt in that situation it would be better not to have a name synonymous with lavatory.) *We had had no word from you and I had been concerned not so much for your immediate family knowing you would arrange for us to hear directly if you were in trouble; but because of Helen and the fearful word from Bristol.* (My mother's eldest sister Helen lived fifteen miles from Bristol). *We realised the South Western City must mean you, but trusted that you were far enough outside to be spared the worst risk. Your feckless young never glance at a paper so they have not worried at all and of course, I have said nothing.*

The children are increasingly well balanced and strong. Blanche sleeps entirely quietly now and during the last week or so has seemed to me much less tense.

Our Christmas turmoil is great and very exciting, with two late evenings and she has gotten through it all beautifully with almost total lack of bickering and high voices. Last Saturday, the day after school broke up there was a lot of rough play and resulting tears but that is all over and I gave various individuals talks on peace in the home and the importance of consideration for others: since then they have all been angels.

On Monday the 22nd we all went to Mt. Holly (erstwhile home of John Woolman, a well known Quaker writer of the 18th century) *about 10 miles away and having an excellent Woolworths Store. There the children did their Christmas shopping and I got things with which to fill their stockings. This is considered a great annual excursion and most important.*

Tuesday we spent doing up presents, except Blanche's dancing class party which was a gay affair (4.30–5.45). The thing that makes a dancing class party different from ordinary dancing class is ice cream instead of lemonade and two prize dances instead of one.

After early supper Dick and the children 'did the rounds', as we call it, which means took our presents around to their proper destinations. When we got back we all trimmed the tree together so it was quite late before I sent them up to undress. They came down in their nighties and we sat around the fire while Dick read the Christmas Chapters; all of us reciting the parts of Luke II that they knew and then we sang carols and I tucked them in bed quite exhausted but entirely happy at almost 10 o'clock. After that I arranged the presents from Dick and me in front of the dining-room fireplace and we got to bed about 1.45a.m.

Yesterday I missed you all day, otherwise our cup was full. Our routine has become tradition. The children are not allowed to get out of bed before 8.00 on Christmas morning. They woke us with carols at 8.30 then we all got dressed. I rushed down and started breakfast: traditionally, grapefruit, sausage, toast, Hartley's marmalade, coffee and milk and was ready to come in and attend the opening of the stockings by the fireplace.

The tree stands in the corner of the dining room. I had gotten various odds and ends at Woolworths for the dolls house for Lou. The stockings were much alike: full of soap and school supplies, oranges, barley sugar, toys, pencils, erasers, notebook paper, hankies, honey and almond cream, toothpaste and such oddments. Besides the stockings were put the presents. Blanche had Mary (her doll) dressed in a new long baby dress and petticoat and oblong work box, cedar lined with green and white flowered paper with a dressing gown in it for Mary made of flowered flannel. Mary was sitting in a high chair and looked beautiful. Also there were pyjamas for B. as well as a book and roller skates.

Lou had a new baby completely dressed, only the trousseau was packed in her pink work box and the baby was asleep in a nice little cot with white sheets and pink rugs. She had on a long white flannelette nightie and was tied at the bottom of the cot so she could not kick off the covers. This baby looks very real, it is made of rubber so is soft to hold and can go in the bath. She has a bottle and lots of diapers and rubber panties, flannel petticoats, white petticoat, fine muslin frock, pink wool sweater and a dressing gown to come.

They nearly had a spasm. I have never seen such joy: Blanche enchanted with Mary and Lou speechless and not able to open her stocking for hugging her doll. Then came your wire at breakfast time and our hearts all went out to you.

I shall never forget the delight of that new and beautifully dressed doll which was all my heart could desire. For all my tomboy play with Richard so much of the time I was girl enough to be absolutely enchanted with this gift.

There follows a long list of all the other presents we received, which was staggeringly long. Gifts from my Mother's brother, my Uncle Vigurs, in New York and also all the Wood relations had included us in their giving. Luckily the presents from England had arrived beforehand and better still no duty demanded, always a worry. These had been kept to add to the celebrations. An embarrassment of riches.

Twenty-four Woods sat down to Christmas dinner at Grandfather Wood's house at Riverton just outside Moorestown. Dick had two younger brothers with families who also joined the festivities. One family lived in Moorestown so we knew them and their two daughters, Peggy and Molly, well because Molly was in Richard and my class at school and Peggy was in Blanche's. The other family also with two

"Old World Refugees Greet 1941 in New World", an Evening paper, Philadelphia

daughters had travelled from Cambridge, Massachusetts

This was a very happy day concluded on our way home by a drive around the town to see all the lighted Christmas trees. Aunt Nancy recalls that Sonny (her pet name for Richard) counted 225. How different from the blackout back home.

She concludes her letter: *I feel very thankful the children have been so happy. I have watched very carefully the last week thinking it would be a hard time but they have thrown themselves into the family routine wholeheartedly and seem happy and gay. They have added greatly to our happiness although my heart has ached for you having them so far away. They are both terribly loveable and we all love them dearly.*

Our love to you all too and wishes for a brighter New Year.

> *Much love*
> *Nancy*

As mentioned my mother had a brother who lived in New York having emigrated to America in the 1920s. He had had a good job in South America with the Inter-national Telegraph and Telephone Company but lost it during the Depression and subsequently had only a modest post with the Postal Telegraph Co. at Radio City, New York. My mother had received the following rather cryptic letter on our arrival in America.

37–28 Eighty-Sixth St
Jackson Heights,
L.I. N.Y.
August 29th 1940

Dear Joan,
Some weeks ago I heard from Helen that you were thinking of sending your children out to the vicinity of Toronto but had made no final decision.

Consequently since I had heard nothing from either of you I was very much surprised to see pictures of Blanche and Joan (he was obviously unaware that I was always called Louise) in one of the New York papers last Monday afternoon. As I told Helen and she no doubt passed the information on to you that I had offered to be whatever help I could short of sponsoring which is, of course impossible. I was very much surprised that you had not asked me to do what I could to welcome them in passing through New York.

You surely could have cabled me when you knew they had left. I could readily found out where to contact them. As it is now I have no information as to where they are or who they are with. I presume of course that they are with Friends in Philadelphia.

If you wish that I may have the opportunity to see them and to let them get know their own relatives in the States you might let me know where they are.

> *Affectionately,*
> *Vigurs*

Uncle Vigurs and his wife Julia had eventually found out our whereabouts and had come to visit us in November 1940. It would appear that the letter my Uncle Vigurs wrote reporting on this visit at the time got lost. However, it is referred to in one of Uncle Dick's rare letters written in February 1941 when Aunt Nancy was away in Florida. And yet another letter telling of the visit arrived much later in March 1941.

For Blanche and myself the outcome was some lovely well thought out presents for both us and the Wood children for Christmas, picking up on what Uncle Vigurs and Aunt Julia had learnt about us all on this visit. Luckily his petulance with his younger sister was not visited on us. I received a big upholstered box full of sewing things; materials, laces, buttons, tiny ostrich feathers, bindings, trimmings and threads. Blanche had a badminton racquet and shuttlecocks as well as a pen and pencil set with international writing paper, an artist's set for Richard who had been drawing a schooner on the day they came, as well as handkerchiefs for Becca and Anne.

When it finally arrived at Tobo, Uncle Vigurs' account of the visit reiterated the news of our successful absorption into a very happy casual household at Moorestown, judging correctly that the Woods looked like good American Quaker stock related to dozens of people in the town. In fact, Aunt Nancy could trace her forebears to one Captain Sam Morris who was involved in the American Revolution in Philadelphia . He was a Friend but because of his participation in the Revolution, was "read" out of the Meeting he was in.

My sister and I apparently regarded this Aunt and Uncle as just another pair of strangers who this time just happened to be related as well, a detail that had little meaning. One can sense that finding us so well settled was accompanied by a big sigh of relief because, as Uncle Vigurs explained, there was no way he could have kept his nieces in his small two bedroom apartment in New York.

What none of these letters hints at is the fact that when Vigurs and Julia arrived at 272 on their visit, Aunt Nancy felt she knew Julia. It had slowly come to her where they had met before. Julia had worked as a maid in her parents house some years earlier and had been dismissed for stealing. Aunt Nancy never told a soul. Five years later, when my mother arrived in America the secret came out and she was told of this revelation. Mind you, my mother did not like Julia, but this had nothing to do with this unknown piece of Julia's history but more to do with the antipathy she had for all the spouses of her brothers and sisters. She was full of irrational prejudices of this sort.

CHAPTER THIRTEEN

Winter 1941

A FTER CHRISTMAS that year the weather was very cold and snowy, a fairly routine event in New Jersey, but for Blanche and myself the snow was much deeper and lasted longer than anything we had ever experienced in the mild climate of the English West Country. This meant frozen lakes and snow for sledding. I always revelled in any physical activity and threw myself into learning to skate with great enthusiasm as my first letter of the New Year reveals.

Dear Mummy and Daddy,

Aunt Nancy, Uncle Dick and Richard are finishing colds. I am staying at Grandmother and Grandfather Wood's so I won't catch one. I have a pair of wonderful ice skates. The roads are frozen and it is hailing. Grandmother doesn't want us to go out. I am resting.

Blanche and Anne went skating the other day before I got my skates. Blanche used me as a towboat and Anne used me as a beaning post.

Did you have a good Xmas and New Year. I expect John loved it. We did not get the apples. I am not at school today as the roads are too slippery.

Love

Louise

The older generation of Woods lived at Riverton which is about five miles from Moorestown. Grandmother Wood was frequently called on to relieve the pressure of family life at 272. She was a plump, friendly and gentle woman who was a benign presence for the whole family. She also financially helped the Wood family by paying for a lot of

Blanche and my clothes as well as our expensive teeth straightening, the complicated arrangement of metal bands and wires put on our teeth to bring them into line.

Even though American cars often featured chains on their wheels in winter months, this was obviously a very icy time with hail falling on snow making the roads ice layered lakes. The snow was eight inches deep and the temperatures down to 16 degrees Fahrenheit below freezing, too cold that stormy day to go out and play. I remember how silent and beautiful the snow made the garden at Riverton, loading each branch with its own canopy of twinkling white while I looked out from indoors just longing to make a snowman out there.

"Oh, Blanche, I do wish we could go out! What I like best is lying on my back in fresh snow to make an angel."

By lying on the ground and working your arms up and down beside you, the pattern in the snow looked like wings and by moving your legs sideways it then looked like a skirt; more angel-like than I would ever be.

Blanche replied; "I would rather go skating again. Do you think the ice will stay on the lake long enough for us to have some more skating when we get back to Moorestown? I would really love to learn to go backwards and then turn and spin."

We all imagined we would be able to spin and skate like Sonja Heinie if we practiced enough; she was the current World Figure Skating Champion.

"Oh, I do want to try out my new skates, too" I yearned. "They are figure skates, you know, with zigzag curves on the front so you can stand on your toes."

The colds mentioned turned into a serious bout of influenza which was laying everyone at 272 very low. A nurse had been imported to look after the invalids as they were all so poorly and in the end the nurse herself succumbed to the high fever and was sent home to recover herself. The 'flu had been so debilitating that it was decided that Aunt Nancy would join Grandfather and Grandmother Wood on holiday in Florida which was warm and tropical at that time of year with a profusion of flowers blossoming, much to Aunt Nancy's delight. Uncle

Dick was unable to join them because of the relentless demands of deadlines entailed in producing "The Friend" magazine week after week. Becca and Richard who had also succumbed to the virulent bug but had returned to school when their strength allowed.

Aunt Nancy off for five weeks of sun and recuperation described herself as being like the Shipwrecked Sailor in A.A.Milne's poem: *There Was An Old Sailor My Grandfather Knew.* She quotes the appropriate verses...

First verse

There was once an old sailor my grandfather knew
Who had so many things he wanted to do
That when ever he thought it was time to begin,
He couldn't because of the state he was in.

Last verse

And so in the end he did nothing at all,
But basked on the shingle wrapped up in a shawl,
And I think it was dreadful the way he behaved
He did nothing but basking until he was saved.

Meanwhile we were looked after by a nurse-cum-housekeeper called Mrs. Keading. Mrs Keading was a stout lady with grey permed hair who did not endear herself to us because as soon as she arrived, she immediately began by nagging us to pick up our clothes and to improve our table manners something that neither Aunt Nancy nor Mother, it would appear, were too strict about. For Blanche, being naturally tidy this was not a problem, but for me it was. My untidiness was illustrated by the shoe episode that happened later.

Getting ready for school one morning I was much distressed.

"I can't find my shoes to wear, anywhere." I complained. "What am I going to do?"

"Has thee looked everywhere?" I was asked .

"Yes, I just don't know where they are."

"Well there is nothing else for it, thee will have to wear thy best 'Sunday-Go-To-Meeting' patent leather slippers." Aunt Nancy decided.

A serious hunt later that day found one pair of shoes in the front hall under a chair by the front door, one pair on the laundry tubs in the kitchen and yet another pair under the bath tub. The bath tub was the cast iron variety that could easily conceal a small pair of shoes. At the same time a completely lost sweater was discovered on a chair in the second floor hall.

During her stay, I fell out with Mrs. Keading in a big way. Not over untidiness but another matter.

"Louise, it's time for you to have a violin practice." she announced after school.

"I don't want to." I responded.

"Yes, you must, because you have not done the work Mr. Pew set you at your last lesson." I was told.

"But I hate practicing! I won't do it! I don't care what Mr. Pew wants. I don't have to just cause you say so."

There ensued a very loud confrontation and fireworks between us as Mrs. Keading chased me around the dining room table insisting on my compliance. The plump Mrs. Keading created quite a spectacle when she tried to catch me as we cavorted with the table between us. I shouting at the top of my voice; "I won't! I won't!"

Richard and Blanche looked on awestruck at my defiance. To think, only the week before Grandmother Wood had commented in a letter to my Mother that I was the easier child! I imagine I capitulated but was clearly unhappy in her care for the next thing that happened was that I painted my face all over with cheap red lipstick resulting in another episode of blotchy rash all over my face, just like the poison ivy.

At the weekly violin lessons Richard and I had achieved only modest results. Aunt Nancy was probably less diligent in getting us to practice. It transpired I had a poor ear but excellent form while Richard had a good ear and poor form. Sadly the talents between us did not seem transferable; Mr. Pew had an uphill task with both of us. I finally abandoned my musical career six months later while Richard, who was more musical than I, carried on longer.

When Aunt Nancy returned in February she reported that Lou and Sonny were 'smouldering' after our time with Mrs. Keading so we were immediately whisked out of the house: Richard for a haircut with

Becca and I to go shopping with her. Mrs. Keading departed, no doubt, with a big sigh of relief, to think the house and children were actually still intact as she shut the front door.

Once Mrs. Keading had left, I showed every sign of homesickness which hitherto had not been remarked on. I started talking about John. Was he big enough to ride the big red tricycle? Did he climb trees in Tobo garden like I used to do? I wondered if he was big enough yet to know that the geese at Dodovens would only chase you if you ran away but not if you stood your ground and said "Boo".

I was alarmed no doubt to think my 'Second Mother' had gone away and left me. These were all symptoms of my temporary unhappiness. I even started talking baby talk. To be abandoned by one mother was a situation I had learned to accept, but by two was just too much.

CHAPTER FOURTEEN

Bombing

ALL THROUGH THE SPRING of 1941 there were references to the air raids and bombing that Plymouth was getting from the Nazis. Aunt Nancy was frequently in a dilemma about what and how much we should be told of what was happening at home. We seemed to be so engrossed in our American life that Plymouth seemed a long way away; we ignored the papers that were to be seen in the house. In March and April 1941 Plymouth experienced many air raids that had a devastating effect and again in the spring of 1944. By the end of the War, 40 churches, as well as civic buildings, libraries, theatres and complete shopping streets had all been destroyed. The whole fabric of the city was destroyed, one third of its property value was lost, so eventually the Germans could boast that the town had been wrecked beyond repair. (See p. 221 "Where the Bombs Fell")

The shops and firms migrated to the suburbs and found houseroom in residential houses or wherever they could. Mutley Plain, which was a peripheral shopping street about a mile from the centre of town, became a very busy shopping place. Private houses became drapery stores or offices. I remember finding our chemist at Elburton in someone's front room when I returned from America and found it very odd in comparison to the elaborate drug store in Moorestown.

A letter from my Mother to her sister Kitty describes one of the worst episodes

Tobo,
Elburton
Plymouth
24th March 1941

Dearest Kitty,
I can't tell you how much I have been wanting to let you know that we are quite safe so far. As far as I know, all the Friends at Mutley (the local Friends Meeting was on Mutley Plain, Plymouth) *the relations and our friends are safe. We only know personally one boy in this village who has died from his wounds from the Thursday night raid. That one seemed to us here at Elburton to be chiefly incendiaries in this district, and it was interspersed with H.Es.* (High Explosives) *But before it was finished it moved forward into Plymouth where they dropped chiefly H.Es. and land-mines. After the raid was over at midnight, the rest of the night and all Friday retarded bombs were exploding. The damage was terrific from what we could see on the Friday morning, but it was not comparable to the damage done on Friday night.*

Both sides of George St., Bedford St., the Guildhall and Lord Mayors Chambers, Princess Square entirely, the Post Office and the greater part of Westwell St. and a lot in Notte St.; Brown Wills and Nicholsons place that supplied the whole of the two counties (Devon and Cornwall) *with groceries, the Western Bus Office and the whole block from Balkwells Chemist Shop round to Trevil St., as well as both sides of Old Town St., the entire length. Then I believe property has been damaged as far as the Octagon.*

All these places I've mentioned are not just injured, they are down to the ground. Francis says that all that can be seen of our Frankfurt Street Shop is the extent of it; nothing else whatever. (This was an Ironmongery and Tool shop owned and run by my grandfather). *Today he is seeking other premises as we happen to have quite a quantity of goods on order that should be arriving soon and can be put at the disposal of the public.*

Most of Friday was spent in saving tomato plants on two neighbouring establishments and on Sunday he and Allan (my conscientious objector cousin doing a reserved occupation instead of military service) *did get to Meeting, for which I was very thankful.*

Of course we have here an influx of people. Paul Beregi bombed out of his house and business came on Saturday morning complete with what supplies and luggage he could save from his cafe. He has put the supplies at my disposal and I am glad of this little extra help in the swollen household. On Thursday before the raids Bruno Schadek (a German Refugee) *arrived to take up his quarters here and to work at the Vineries, so we are very full and busy.*

But on Saturday at the end of a completely hectic day the two Keller-ways (he was Manager of the Frankfurt St. Shop) *and two friends walked in and asked for floor space. What an airing of available blankets and lilos. They went before breakfast. In the midst of this our coal is appalling and the cook and heat oven refuses to work. No gas; but light thank goodness.*

There have been three day raids since the Friday night one and retarded bombs are in every direction from here to the other side of no-where. The main road seems to pass our gate via Plympton and the dear old bridge is still unhurt. (The bridge mentioned was the Laira Bridge over the River Plym which we crossed to get to Plymouth from the east. It was "Dear" to Mother because a forebear engineer had built it so she took a proprietorial interest in it.) *I can't tell you of casualties, no one has any authentic rumour about them; but they must be extremely heavy.*

My own personal loss though extremely small does hurt a bit. It was the little occasional chair of Mother's that used to be covered in green buttoned velvet that was having a new loose cover made for it in town. And two weeks laundry of sheets and towels. This must be all for now. We are amazingly well and feel that very soon we shall get our second wind. Do not move us with your sympathy, we know of it and are thankful. John is beautifully fit and slept through everything and that for me beyond his safety was the chief thing.

> *Our very dear love to you,*
> Joan

Reading this and knowing my mother in later years, I am amazed at how stoically she took this situation. In later life she always made a great "to do" about any unusual state of affairs and was guaranteed to magnify the event for greatest drama. Perhaps because this required no embellishments to gain effect it was left to speak for itself.

I have not mentioned the shop, F.T.B. Lawson Ltd., before. This tool and hardware shop was my Grandfather Lawson's first business. He had been trained as an ironmonger and only took up tomato growing after marriage and contact with his wife's Guernsey relations. It was a prosperous enterprise and benefited from providing the Devonport Naval Dockyard with tools. I was never quite sure how my father justified this with his pacifist views, my grandfather on the other hand, as a Methodist and shrewd businessman, was perhaps a little less concerned. Nevertheless, he was sympathetic to Friends' views because, after all, he had sent his son to Leighton Park Quaker School.

For us children the shop had the added advantage of having a toy department. Unfortunately its concentration on toy cars and railway engines benefited brother John more than us girls.

A letter from Aunt Nancy at the end of April tells of her response to these events.

272 West Main Street
Moorestown,
New Jersey

Dear Joan,
I'm sorry I missed writing earlier last week, Your letter was such a relief telling about the bad raid; but you may feel both shocked and relieved about the children's reaction. They have seemingly no realisation that raids can be any worse than those they experienced. We told them that Mr. Richardson's school (Rocky Hill Preparatory School, our old school) *was gone, and Lou was quite sympathetic but Blanche was quite delighted; very joyfully told everyone she saw for the next two days. They are sorry about Grandpa's Shop but your way of telling them about that did not make them think of it as a calamity. They shout with joy at the thought of John licking spoons at the Jam Centre. What an undertaking*

*that will be. I was so thankful that no bodily hurt had come to your
group.*

No mention came through about whether anyone was hurt when the
school was bombed. What a mercy we were not there. It was, of course,
these events that we had gone to escape, so in this respect my parents
will have been relieved to know we were in a much safer place in
Moorestown.

The whole of America was increasingly concerned at the plight of
Britain in the face of all this bombing and Blanche became involved
with a fund raising event that took place in Philadelphia. The above
letter continues:

> *Two of our best actors, Lynn Fontaine and Alfred Lunt have been giving
> special benefit performances for the benefit of British Relief and some good
> soul thought it would be nice for 3 British children to present a bouquet in
> thanks. A friend of mine, working on the Committee asked if Blanche
> could help. I accepted and later when I told Dick he was very irate. How-
> ever, it was too late then and I sent B. off with the ends of her hair curled
> up a bit, not too much, and wearing her best new suit and blouse. She went
> to lunch first with Cora Greenwood, my friend, and the other children and
> then they went backstage to Miss Fontaine's dressing room and presented
> the flowers. Miss Fontaine gave each of them a lovely book autographed by
> her and her husband and a picture. It was a pleasant little ceremony, very
> dignified, but comfortable.*
>
> > *Much love and many thanks for your letters,*
> > *Nancy*

Blanche has vivid memories of this day and still treasures the book and
picture she was given.

CHAPTER FIFTEEN

Sunday school

S UNDAYS, OR FIRST DAY as it was frequently called by Quakers then, always meant Sunday School and Meeting, unless one was ill or elsewhere. There was no question that this is what happened on Sundays followed by Sunday lunch. In England my parents made a practice of inviting other Friends who attended the meeting home to join in that lunch especially if they were visiting from another meeting. It was from amongst the other worshippers that my parents often drew the people for their social activities and Sunday lunch was their main social event of the week. Inviting friends with a large "F" or small "f" for an evening meal, as might happen today, was a much less frequent occurrence. While in Moorestown hospitality would more often involve a grown up dinner in the evening when Blanche and Anne would be called on to wait at table.

Louise and Blanche, 1941. Wearing Liberty prints made by Mother

The meeting house we went to in Moorestown was next to our school, not quite a mile further eastwards along Main Street. It was a classical style one storey building in red brick purpose built as a meeting house with square windows quite high up in the walls so you could not see out when seated inside. No distractions of watching the outside world when you should be taking part in the religious meeting of the week. Our Meeting was attended by what was known as "Orthodox Friends" but there was another meeting house on the other side of the school which was attended by "Hicksite Friends" who were more evangelical and had broken with main stream Friends during the 19th century. Both groups had reasonably sized congregations but later after my return home they became re-united.

In our meeting house in Moorestown the main room where we gathered for worship had hard wooden benches on which we sat in lines facing the front of the hall. At the front there was a raised podium on which the elders sat, facing the main body of worshippers, where they kept a benevolent eye on the proceedings. The meeting room itself was quite plain with no ornamentation of any sort to be seen nor any religious symbols. Nothing for children trying to sit still and silent to enjoy looking at by way of a diversion.

The meeting for worship which is the centre of Quaker life, starts in total silence where those participating will hope for a direct experience of God. The silence continues until such time as one of the meeting feels inspired to speak on a matter of concern which he or she feels would be helpful to those present in their search for divine guidance. Originally the name, Quakers, was given to Friends because it was not uncommon in the early days of the Society of Friends for those who spoke to shake. I certainly can remember seeing those participating in vocal ministry shaking though I must admit I always considered it an attack of nerves rather than divine intervention!

When all the Wood family went to "First Day Worship" Uncle Dick would frequently be one of the elders sitting facing while the rest of us would sit in the body of the hall. How we sat along a bench was strictly controlled by our elders and betters. Richard and I were never allowed to sit beside each other or next to Blanche but were carefully disposed between Aunt Nancy, Becca and Anne to ensure that no whisperings or little games could take place between us. Though American meetings are rarely totally silent the periods of silence could seem interminable to us younger ones, not helped by the hardness of the wooden benches.

After an hour we would watch diligently for the worthy Friends sitting in front to shake hands, signalling the conclusion of the period of worship. Afterwards we might compare notes.

"Richard, did you see the old man next to Uncle Dick fall so fast asleep I thought his head would fall off?"

Sunday school in England had taken place at the same time as the adults' silent meeting for worship and we children only joined it by creeping quietly in at the back for the last fifteen minutes, whereas in New Jersey we had an hour of Sunday school before adult Meeting. In the American Sunday school we often had stories of past exploits of Friends or learnt about famous Quakers from history. People such as George Fox, the Founder of Quakerism, and Elizabeth Fry the social reformer who did much to help improve the life of women prisoners in London in the early 19th century. Then there were those tales from the early days in America of the bravery of Friends in the face of savage Indians where the pacifist approach had won respect which I have already referred to.

In Philadelphia there was a rich Quaker heritage to draw on, starting with William Penn himself, who had established Pennsylvania and the "City of Brotherly Love", John Woolman, a Quaker thinker and writer, John Greenleaf Whittier the poet and hymn writer and a number of others. John Woolman, whose birthplace was near Moorestown at Mt. Holly, had worked hard in the 18th century to discourage people in the Northern States from keeping slaves. Friends were staunch Abolitionists from as early as the 1760s and there were exciting stories of the "Underground Railroad" we learned about.

The Underground Railroad was a secret pre-arranged route along which runaway slaves fleeing cruel masters in the south of the country were passed from one safe house to another by sympathisers until they reached the safety of Canada, or the Northern States. Quite often

Friends would provide these safe houses along the route at considerable risk to themselves; the penalties for participation in this illegal network were very severe. It is considered that 75,000 slaves were freed this way before the Civil War broke out. The state of Ohio was closely involved with these activities because the Ohio River provided the longest border with the Southern States and slaves could cross here and find their way to cities like Chicago and Detroit.

We would also discuss the current world situation and how Friends with their strong belief in pacifism should respond to the War. As mentioned earlier, my father was a pacifist and registered as a conscientious objector, though his stand did not make a lot of difference to his situation because he was already in a the reserved occupation of growing food. Uncle Dick was also a pacifist but at this time was over draft age.

Quakers, though not fighting, worked hard in many other areas to do what they could to reduce the conflict and to relieve the suffering of those caught up in the War. We were early instilled with a social conscience and of finding ways to help others, especially those less well off than ourselves. This is well illustrated by a letter that my mother received from my Sunday school teacher, Marian Haines. I am quite embarrassed at its content as I sound such a little prig, but in fact I feel it must be taken as an example of how this concern for others was nurtured in us.

Marian Haines was a kind and homely woman with no makeup and plain hairstyle who wore sensible clothes and shoes. She was a warmhearted person who as this letter shows, gave us freedom of expression in her lessons.

124 E. MainStreet
Moorestown, N.J.
Nov.5 1941

Dear Mrs. Lawson,
My reason for writing is to tell you of a very heartening experience which I had at First-Day School last First-Day. Louise and Richard are in my class, and Rachel Cadbury thought you would like to hear what took place as a result of Louise's unusual wisdom and understanding. The class is a

fine group of six boys and seven girls. Michael Rutter (another evacuee) is in it too, as it is a combination of 4th and 5th Graders.

We had been making plans about spending our collection. In thinking of what was needed, or what would be a suitable Christmas gift, butter to England was suggested. We found out that it would take more than half our money to send one small package. We wondered what to do and suggested sending one package to Michael's family at Christmas and to Louise's at Easter. Then one of the children mentioned the chocolate covered vitamin pills which are being sent to some children in the South of France. A worker from the Friends Service Committee had told them about the children who didn't know how milk tasted. Then another child spoke for some of our needs at home. What should we do? There were many suggestions.

We decided not to vote, but to talk over our ideas the way grown-ups do at Monthly Meeting. At this point Louise said: "I don't think we should send the butter to England. It wouldn't be helping enough people. It is too much like a teacher having favourites. I think the Service Committee would know best where our money is needed and that we should give it to them." Michael readily agreed.

Those children wanted us all to think of others and give to others as a group and not their families. You can guess that I was touched by their sense of vision and the clear way in which Louise expressed what she felt was right. After this it was decided to let the Service Committee choose where our money was most needed; "Even if it is in Africa." Richard Wood said.

I am so glad to know Louise and hope I may meet her parents sometime.
Sincerely,
E. Marian Haines

My parents also heard about the "Butter Story" from another source, which again illustrates the network of contacts amongst Friends. It was relayed by Jack Cadbury whose parents lived in Moorestown but who worked for the Friends War Victims Relief Committee based at Friends House in London and was known to my mother and father.

In his work he was able to cross the Atlantic between the United

From left: Anne Wood, Richard Wood, Nancy Wood, Louise Lawson, Blanche Lawson and Rebecca Wood

States and England even though the War was restricting travel for most people.

There are several letters from Jack as he became a link between the two families; visiting Blanche and me in Moorestown and my parents in Plymouth. The first written from London relates messages from us to our parents particularly from Blanche to say that Miss Swan is being very kindly and that they grade schools differently in America than in England. She is letting her hair grow and has many new dresses. She sends her love to John. I reported that I had a new monkey named "Chatter" (not a real monkey, I hasten to add) and had painted a picture of Pooh Bear in art class. He reports that Blanche's reading is improving and that we sent our love to our Grandparents as well. We also wanted to know if Florrie our much loved maid at Tobo, had left or not.

It was Jack's mother, Rachel Cadbury with whom my mother became friends when she visited Moorestown to collect us after the War. The next letter from Jack, dated 8th July 1941, is sent to my parents after a visit to Plymouth when he was able to report on a visit to 272 first hand. He writes: *'In these times, and especially in your case, there is a flourishing in this island of a kind of spontaneous and genuine fellowship. I felt is so keenly with you and I shall never forget or lose it. Perhaps this is one of the best things the war has done, for it turns the defeat of war into a victory of human brotherhood and understanding.'*

It is later in December of that year when he also reports on the Sunday School "Butter" incident. It illustrates well how we were encouraged in Quaker beliefs. There is no doubt that this Quaker upbringing in America and England strongly influenced my life. It was a very sheltered life and it was only later when I went to University, swelled in numbers by ex-servicemen, that I began to learn what life was like outside the Quaker close community with its strict set of standards.

CHAPTER SIXTEEN

Lake Eaglesmere

ONCE SCHOOL HAD finished at the beginning of June 1941 we had the prospect of three glorious months of vacation to look forward to before school started again after Labour Day in early September. What freedom! Summers in New Jersey could be very hot and humid; temperatures in the nineties were not uncommon. Looking back now I am surprised how we learned to live in this heat without the air-conditioning that is freely available today.

That first year it was decided to escape to Lake Eaglesmere in the Appalachian Mountains of Pennsylvania for some of that time. A family uncle owned a cottage beside the lake which he liked to use in July and August when it could be even hotter down on the Plain, but it did mean it was available for Aunt Nancy's "flock" as she called us, in June. We all of us were to go except Uncle Dick; he apparently hated mountains, but anyway his magazine deadlines made it rather difficult for him to join us. The suggestion that Uncle Dick did not like mountains I feel was rather a travesty because on other occasions he enjoyed memorable holidays in the Adirondacks in New York State.

By this small lake at Eaglesmere there was a little village and a few hotels mostly not open until July with scattered cottages hidden in the woods. The description in the letters tell us that the lake is in the peak of a mountain, perhaps an ancient crater, filled with crystal clear spring water and woods which come down to the waters edge. At one end there was a white sand beach, lovely for swimming and well guarded, while the rest of the shore was rocky. Laurel and rhododendron were everywhere and the woods were full of wild flowers. This was a real wilderness and it did not need a great stretch of the imagination to picture Red Indians stalking through the woods carrying their bows and arrows, hunting for deer.

Our cottage was only about 100 feet from the shore so our days were spent swimming and boating. Blanche, Richard and I could all swim after a fashion before that holiday but were much improved by the end. I remember having over ambitious ideas of how I could swim and was hauled out spluttering from deep water by a life-guard.

"Come on, young lady, back to shallow water until you can swim properly," I was told.

"I know I can do it next time, watch me," I responded; I had no fear.

Despite our limited swimming skill we were allowed out in the row-boat and Indian canoe. We were restricted to within 25 feet of the shore where it was shallow enough for us to stand. I think Aunt Nancy was working on the same principal as the father of the Swallows in the Arthur Ransome books who, when asked if they could go out in a boat, cabled the reply, "BETTER DROWNED THAN DUFFERS IF NOT DUFFERS WONT DROWN." We spent hours learning how to row and paddle, though there is a comment that Blanche was too full of her own knowledge to be easily taught. However, she managed it somehow.

As avid readers of Arthur Ransome, we were well versed in the stories of the Swallows and Amazons and we wanted to sail like them. One day, once we had mastered rowing Richard said to me; "Lou, I think we ought to fix the rowboat with a sail."

"That's a swell idea." I replied. "How can we make a mast and fit a sail?" I wanted to know.

We set about it finding a pole for a mast and then Richard said, "I know, we could use that big stripy bath towel for the sail".

Low and behold, we got it to work, Richard in the stern using an oar for a rudder and I in the bow manning the sheets or sail lines. Its best sailing position was with the wind astern so we looked just like a Chinese junk scudding down the lake.

Aunt Nancy had a very relaxed approach to our exploits and we were allowed great freedom in our activities. This attitude we were aware was not the result of indifference, but more an expectation on her part that if she trusted us we would respond by behaving responsibly and by not getting into dangerous situations beyond our capabilities. I think she also trusted the Good Lord to keep an eye on us as well.

Soon after our arrival numbers were increased by a group of Becca's just graduated 17 year old friends from school arriving for a house party. They were celebrating the end of their College Boards (entrance exams). Such a throng meant a lot of work so Aunt Nancy's hairdresser's Lithuanian mother had been engaged to help with the cooking during this holiday, added to that we were all allocated jobs to do each day to lighten the load. My tasks were to sweep the porch and then collect the water from the spring. We drank spring water that was fresh and pure, water that is probably put in bottles today and sold for a high price. The others all had their tasks too, laying or clearing table or fetching supplies from the shop. Part of American culture includes a vision of the homesteader 's children pitching in and helping with the chores, though in the olden days it probably meant feeding the calves or milking the cows.

Picnics were the other great delight, frequently taken beside a mountain stream where the fast flowing waters would be rushing down the slope looking for a way between the big boulders. I loved nothing better than leaping about on these rocks finding a way to the other side.

As Aunt Nancy said, "Lou has a God-given gift for falling in the water." On one occasion I even fell in with my emergency clothes on and had to go home with someone else's sweater on my top half and another on my bottom half, using the arms for trouser legs.

Going home after the picnic could be special too, if it was just getting dark we would see the deer beginning to move after a day of hiding in the woods. Their elegant shapes, heads up and ears pointing with bright eyes caught in the car headlights at the roadside. It would be a game to see how many we could see.

We were still taken to Meeting even though we were on vacation.

We went to an old fashioned wooden meeting house with the usual hard wooden benches to sit on. The ladies toilets here were quite remarkable. The far wall in a small room had a long bench along the far wall with round holes at intervals all the way along it. The bench seat with the holes was aligned over holes in the ground below floor level. We all sat down together side by side, no modesty here. I remember with awe being there on one occasion when a rather plump and elderly Friend rushed in, divested herself of her knickers and sat down heavily exclaiming, "Oh, what a relief, our friend Samuel did go on so."

Wherever we were, at home in Moorestown or on vacation, reading out loud was always an evening occupation. That year it was *Lorna Doone* which we all loved and certainly Blanche and I could picture because Exmoor is similar to the Dartmoor we knew about from our home in Devon.

CHAPTER SEVENTEEN

The long hot summer and summer camp

PLANS FOR OUR OCCUPATION during the rest of the long vacation after our trip to Eaglesmere were carefully laid. It had been agreed that I would go to summer camp in August, something I was thrilled to do. It was a common experience for American children to be sent away to summer camp during the long holiday, a practice that was not known in England at that time. The original plan was for me to go for four weeks paid for by the Friends Service Committee while Richard, on a Woods budget, was to go for only two weeks in July followed by a trip to Maine visiting a school friend.

Blanche was asked to join a school friend, who was an only child, for a holiday in July also in Maine, but she could not decide whether she would like to join me at Dark Waters Camp afterwards. Aunt Nancy was anxious that she make up her own mind whether to go or not. As mentioned, New Jersey was very hot and steamy during July and August so anyone who could, would try and escape to somewhere cooler. Maine was an ideal vacation land with cooler temperatures a beautiful rocky coastline, occasional sandy beaches and inland, wild forests with many lakes hidden in the pine trees, often warmer for swimming than the very cold waters off the coast. I heard all about it when she returned.

Aunt Nancy and Uncle Dick were themselves hoping to escape to the New Jersey shore in August and they were not sure that Blanche would enjoy being there rather than Dark Waters Camp after her Maine trip. They envisaged her complaining endlessly about the mosquitoes and flies which obviously came next to spiders in her list of bêtes noir. Nevertheless, about this time Blanche began conquering her fear of spiders. She was seen walking out the door with a piece of screwed up paper saying as she went: "I am just carrying out a spider I found."

Added to that there was a danger of hearing the "I've Nothing to Do" refrain because the adults did things like read, bird watch and paint while on holiday; not activities to enthral a girl of eleven. However, the decision was left in hopes that pragmatism on Blanche's part might prevail.

While Richard and Blanche were away in July, I enjoyed playing with my girlfriends from school. We all cycled to each others houses around the town. My main friends were Mary Joy Archer, Lois Farrell, Janet Haines, Margaret Caldwell, Kirby Thompson and others as well. From this it can be seen that by now I was well integrated with my class. Mary Joy and Lois were both sporty like me and we would join games of softball with the boys. Later Dorothy Porter and Esther Wilson who joined the school after I did also became good friends of mine. The latter was the owner of a much enjoyed horse.

Softball is baseball with a larger softer ball and rules similar to our English Rounders. The version we played we called "Workies Up" where, instead of having two sides which meant having more people than were usually around, we would have a system of moving the players in a specific order according to their game position. As soon as someone was out, they would have to go to the far outfield, the least loved position. From here you would have to work your way up through the fielding positions until you reached the best one, i.e. the hitter, once more. Thus the "catcher" (the backstop in our English rounders) would become the hitter (batsman), the pitcher (cf. bowler) became the catcher, the person on first base became the pitcher, the person on second base moved to first and so on; ensuring everyone would get a slice of the action in turn.

I remember Lois had older brothers and had learnt to throw the ball overarm very well. I learnt too so that when I came back to England and played rounders I always ended up fielding in the out field because

I could throw it far. Of course when Richard and his friends were around they played it too. Richard fancied himself as a catcher and had a special padded glove for catching a real baseball. I spent many hours throwing the ball to him to help him improve his skills.

Or, in total contrast, I would join in the sewing that Becca and Anne were doing that summer when they were learning to use the electric sewing machine. My effort was in order to dress my dolls. Holiday time was often an opportunity for reading aloud especially when there was a quiet activity like sewing taking place; no television then! "Alice Through the Looking Glass" was one of the books we all enjoyed that time.

There is a lovely note in a letter dated that July to say that Chatter, the monkey, was not a live monkey. Aunt Nancy wrote. *"I bought it for Lou as a sort of consolation prize when she had voluntarily confessed to a sin and gone through the requisite very difficult and embarrassing necessity of making good her misdemeanour like a little soldier."* Chatter was only 12–14 inches high and rather like a Teddy Bear, only he had a very sleepy smile and half shut eyes. *"He is very nice to hug in bed. Lou has knit him a charming yellow sweater and loves him dearly."* Aunt Nancy continued. Of my sin I have no recollection. My high spirits frequently got me into trouble but this sounded a bit more serious than the usual. Chatter on the other hand is well remembered and was my constant companion for many years.

Between times there would be picnics and outings, while the housework was left undone. One such outing was a trip to the Zoo taking Emma, the maid with her daughter, Geneva. Her naming I believe coincided with events linked to the development of the League of Nations. Geneva went to the Public School at Moorestown, the antithesis of an English Public School, where most children in town went to school who did not go Moorestown Friends Schools. The two schools were friendly rivals. Geneva was about Anne's age and buxom like her Mother. She fascinated me because she was so much more streetwise than the rest of us. "Streetwise" was not a term used in those days but it describes well the difference between us. For instance, she began wearing makeup and nail varnish at a very early age. Makeup was definitely frowned on at 272, being considered most un-Quakerly and

Blanche and Louise playing in the garden in summer, 1943

pandering to female vanities. Similarly my own mother always tut-tutted when I wore lipstick even as a University student

The Zoo trip included all the fun of seeing those wild animals from exotic parts of the world, but best of all the monkeys and the chimpanzees that Blanche had seen on her birthday trip the previous Fall. In a world without T.V. and today's nature programmes, these animals would only have been seen in picture books.

In the event, when Blanche returned from Maine, the decision about camp was quickly made (I'm not quite sure by whom) and she was hurriedly packed up so we could both go to camp together. This meant there was a frenzy of sewing on name tapes on all her clothes to be taken, mine having already been done. She had returned from Maine glowing with health, inches taller and rounder, carrying reports on what a good guest she had been. They had stayed in a log cabin so the lack of modern facilities like plumbing and electricity had been conquered hence the thought of summer camp was now less daunting. Other excitements had been seeing a moose and a spectacular show of

Cabins at Camp Dark Waters

the Northern lights or Aurora Borealis. Being with others her own age was now much more appealing than being the only youngster down at 'The Shore'.

Camp Dark Waters (still running today) was only five miles from Moorestown on the side of Rancocas Creek. A creek coloured deep red-brown from the cedar trees which lined its banks. The water colour was reminiscent of the peat coloured streams that run off Dartmoor in Devon. The countryside was miles of unbroken pine forest with occasional clearings growing on the infertile sands of the New Jersey Coastal Plain.

At camp we lived in cabins sleeping eight girls in each. Junior Counsellors were allocated to each cabin to keep an eye on us, usually older teenagers earning vacation money. These girls were fun and easy to talk to which helped make the holiday a happy experience. Activities like meals and indoor games took place in large purpose built buildings on site. Life was organised from an early morning reveille bugle call to wake us up, right through the day to the final bugle call for lights out at bedtime. The list of activities was endless, swimming, tennis, canoeing, nature classes, craft work, outdoor cooking and lots besides. We loved it, swimming three times a day, keeping cool in the heavy heat of

July, cooking out doors over campfires with singsongs afterwards. The songs we sang soon became familiar like "Oh My Darling Clementine", "She'll Be Coming Round the Mountain When She Comes", quite a different selection to the ones sung during that air raid at Euston. Living outdoors as we did, we enjoyed the fireflies that came out at dusk flashing their little florescent lamps in the gathering dark. It was fun to try and catch them, but if you put them in a jar the magic was gone.

When I got back to Moorestown I was full of my escapades.

"Aunt Nancy do you know what I did? I jumped off the high board at the swimming pool and the horseback-riding was really swell, and do you know I was allowed to canter with a leading rein. I was the only one in my group to do that." Quite intrepid for a new adventure.

Blanche had enjoyed it just as much and had got (I nearly said gotten) her name on a special plaque for helpfulness. News we imparted at the tops of our voices.

"Girls, girls, please don't shout so, I can't bear it." Aunt Nancy found our loud voices and noisiness one of the hardest things to endure. At this time it was emphasised by the fact that she had been having a quiet time in our absence.

My family maintains that we still shout and when my sister and I speak over the phone we hardly need the help of the telephone wires for us to hear each other, one in Cambridge and the other in Devon.

CHAPTER EIGHTEEN

The shore

THE LAST WEEKEND OF AUGUST, the weekend that really marked the end of the summer vacation, was to be spent down on the New Jersey Atlantic Coast. The family borrowed a small cottage from Aunt Nancy's friend Agnes Stokes. Aunt Nancy, Uncle Dick and the older girls were already there and Blanche and I were to join them once our camping vacation had finished. Richard arrived from visiting his friend Daniel Collins in Maine. Remarkably Richard at the age of nine had made this round trip of six hundred and fifty miles all on his own, on a through train from Philadelphia to Newport Junction, Maine including two meals in the dining car each way. No doubt helpful car attendants on the train kept an eye on him. A really grand adventure.

Cottage on New Jersey Shore

His friend Daniel Collins was the youngest in a very rich family and his older siblings were lots older than he was. Indicative of this wealth was the fact that he had a governess as well as more than one pony to ride. I was very impressed by this. It was the governess who on his return prepared Richard for joining us at the Jersey Shore, for that last weekend, via Grandmother Wood who put him on the train to Seaside Park to meet the rest of us. Grandmother was frequently called in to help on the domestic scene whether it was like this in providing another pair of hands or to provide an alternative home as she had when there was flu at 272 in the winter. She also had been called on to rescue Blanche when she had been taken ill at camp and was in need of some individual nursing while Aunt Nancy and Uncle Dick were already ensconced down at the Shore.

I am amazed reading the letters that it was only a long weekend we spent at the seaside on this occasion because it was so memorable and we had such a good time that I find it hard to believe it was so short. However, over the years we had other trips there to reinforce the first experience.

We stayed in a small wooden cottage perched on a high dune on a lonely stretch of beach. The beach was on the ocean side of a long thin peninsular off the coast of New Jersey. One of the exciting things about the drive down this long thin stretch of land along a bumpy gravel private road was that we were allowed to ride on the outside of the big old car, standing on the running board with the wind blowing through our hair and hanging on like the gangsters of old.

The little house, reached from the road by a boardwalk across the dunes had quite a job fitting in seven of us. Every room was slept in including the kitchen where Richard was camped down, but this just added to the fun. Sadly this little wooden house perched high on the dunes was washed away years later in a winter storm.

A far-reaching length of white sand was all that could be seen in two directions with the blue ocean piling up a succession of breaking waves changing from blue to green to white surf as the water crashed down and ran up the beach. The fascination was the forever changing mood of the sea from day to day; some days gently lapping the sand with hardly any swell to be seen, on others great rollers that could pull you off your feet with strength in the undertow after they had spent themselves on the beach with a thundering crash. If it was like that we had to hold hands for safety when jumping over the waves or, as we got bigger and braver, learning to dive through them just at the right moment as they curled over to break. Mistakes in timing were paid for dearly as you would get severely rolled around hardly knowing which way was up or when your next breath of air could be found amongst the white swirling water; the possible danger of getting it wrong made it more exciting.

Behind the cottage was "The Bay" which separated the beach from the mainland about five miles away. This was brackish, sluggish and shallow, edged by rushes and reeds in many places and low scrub behind in complete contrast to the ocean side. Here was the home of the flies and mosquitoes which could be such a nuisance if the wind was coming from the west across The Bay. The Bay was crossed by narrow wooden bridges that would take you to the small settlements along the peninsular and chain of islands to the south such as Seaside Park. Today those bridges are strong concrete structures and the easier accessibility which this allows means that the wonderful remoteness we enjoyed has gone.

Richard and I used our time making a boat. I daresay we used things like old orange boxes and driftwood to hammer these constructions together. Uncle Dick and Blanche were pressed into helping us launch it in the Bay. Unfortunately it sank when the right way up but it floated well when upside down so this became the preferred orientation.

Richard loved reading about boats and in particular the stories of the fishermen off New England braving treacherous waters with shoals and fog to fish on the Grand Banks off Newfoundland – the same fog I had experienced on my voyage to America in 1940.

These stories included tales of daring by the U.S. Coast Guard so from this it was a small step to become interested in the coast guard who were active along the New Jersey shore. Our unseaworthy craft was meant to be a "Coast Guard Rescue Boat" in which we were going to perform dashing acts of heroism rescuing ships in distress but the maiden voyage rather dampened that prospect. We settled instead to doing beach patrols monitoring the vessels out at sea or in the bay.

With so much activity between swims and picnics it was no wonder the days went so quickly.

While we were on these escapades the older members would read avidly. They had arrived with a great pile of books to read. *Little Dorrit* and *Quentin Durward* were read aloud to Becca and Anne, while Aunt Nancy was also reading books on Luther, Leonardo and Botticelli as well as books on Louis XI of France and James I of Scotland. The one she had not quite tackled was the *"Essence of Spiritual Religion"* by Elton Trueblood, Uncle Dick's fellow Editor from "The Friend". Is it any wonder that Blanche who wasn't a great reader felt overwhelmed by these swathes of culture.

Louise, Blanche, Richard and Woozer in the summer of 1941 at "The Shore"

CHAPTER NINETEEN

The letters

FTER A YEAR WITH THE WOODS, Blanche and I were very much part of the family, never feeling we were being treated in any way differently from the rest of their children. However, I knew I was not really of the family not least because of the steady flow of letters coming from my home in Devon. Letters and parcels got through remarkably well considering the War raging in Europe and across the Atlantic. The fastest was air mail that could take as little as thirteen days but more commonly it took three or even four weeks while surface mail often took the same amount of time, though more often longer. At worst a letter could take five or even six weeks. There was a continuing debate about whether to use surface or air mail and often, because air mail was more expensive, surface mail would be used. Having arrived in Philadelphia on 30th August 1940, by 26th September Blanche was complaining we had had only two letters in the first month but then the following week three had turned up all at once. This became a not uncommon occurrence.

Always during our stay in America the post was erratic and unreliable. The longer the time a letter took the more difficult it was to get or give a response to anything said earlier that could still seem relevant, whereas if it came quickly we felt much closer. Aunt Nancy philosophically decided in the face of a very long silence on one occasion which made her wonder if there had been a disaster in Plymouth, that someone outside the family would notify her by cable should anything serious have happened, working on the principle that "no news is good news". Many of the letters reaching England from America had been opened and read by censors; though none shows any evidence of having information blanked out, it is possible some were never delivered. There was certainly nothing that could have been construed as subversive in any of them. One envelope remains without the letter enclosed which was written by my mother to Anne. It had a label stuck on it with the

Returned envelope

inscription "Returned to Sender By the Censor – For reason explained in memorandum enclosed in this cover".

All in all my parents received more than two hundred letters, Aunt Nancy averaging a letter at least every two weeks, my sister and I many fewer. I am sure that my mother will have written just as many if not more in the opposite direction. The occurrence of letters from either Uncle Dick or my father was quite rare. Uncle Dick wrote three letters in all, each time to my father, either thanking him for sending money or a Christmas present such the *Countryman Magazine* and *Christian News Letter*.

They mention having received letters from my father but generally it is difficult to judge how many letters he actually wrote as he left the task of keeping in touch to my mother. Blanche in particular begs him to write on several occasions in her letters but to no avail it would seem. There is a letter from her in November 1944 during her last year in America while she is at boarding school at Westtown when she writes what a wonderful treat it was to get a letter from "my father".

One of the reasons for the dearth of letters from my father was that he did not enjoy writing probably due to what today we would call dyslexia. In his work he had little recourse to do much writing and if he did there was usually a secretary on hand who would do it for him. Even in this situation he was not very articulate. There is a story in the

Dear 'Mr. Smith',
It depends how deep you dig.
          Yours sincerely,
                    Francis Lawson

Meanwhile there was still the problem of the unreliability of our letters. This could be compounded by the fact that we would write letters and put them on Aunt Nancy's desk, expecting them to be posted with her next epistle to Devon, but in practice they were likely to become swamped in the hopeless "catch-all" of papers that were piled there and got overlooked for several days. My mother who, like Blanche, was meticulously tidy, would not have been pleased, nor understood living like this.

Besides letters, parcels were also exchanged and to begin with my mother tried to send clothes for us because she was aware of the cost of keeping such a large family clad. She also tried to send more small parcels so if they did not get through less was lost. However, because we were growing all the time, Blanche more than I, this was not always successful as she could not always judge what size was right; also the clothes we wore in America were less formal in subtle ways than those we would be wearing in England.

There was the added complication that parcels could attract customs duty. On one occasion a pair of pyjamas with some knickers cost $4.38 in duty which was considered much too much even though they were joyfully received by my sister and me. Strangely, Anne tells me, Viyella material from these pyjamas is still used, 60 years later, by her to wrap her Christmas tree balls in their storage from year to year!

On the other hand beautifully sewn handkerchiefs which were sent to Becca and an equally beautiful small bag for Aunt Nancy were particularly appreciated as my mother was such an expert needlewoman. They were much treasured. The best piece of sewing my mother sent was a round embroidered panel showing the Pilgrim Fathers leaving for America from the Mayflower Steps in Plymouth. The design which she will have done herself, shows the *Mayflower,* the boat in which the Pilgrims sailed, in Sutton Pool in Plymouth Harbour with the Pilgrims awaiting embarkation beside a jettied mediaeval house still to be seen

at the Barbican today. Behind can be
seen the rolling hills of Dartmoor
and in the corner our house
Tobo. Mother wrote:

> *I am hoping that sometime*
> *towards the end of next month*
> *you will receive a package*
> *from me. It is my version of*
> *the "Sailing of the Mayflower*
> *from the Barbican at Ply-*
> *mouth" and on that account may*
> *have some point for you who have*
> *sheltered my daughters; only they are*
> *neither Dutch nor persecuted Dissenters.*
>
> *It has been a joy to me to prepare this peice of*
> *embroidery for you and it comes with my dearest love and is a thank offering.*
> *Though Victorian in style I hope it may not offend your artistic sense in any*
> *way. Joan Lawson.*

It is now in Anne's care with the prospect of eventually going to a
Philadelphia museum.

Equally, my sister and I would send items back to England for
Christmas and other events like birthdays. I remember working long
and hard to knit a red jumper for brother, John, which I struggled to
finish over a long period of time. I was lucky that when it was finally
done a Dr. Melville Mackenzie passed through 272 on his way to England and was able to take it with him to ensure its safe delivery. Years
later my brother told me he never wore it because he could not even
get it over his head! One exchange that continued long after our return
was the custom of the Woods sending the Lawsons the *Atlantic Monthly*
and the Lawsons reciprocating with the *The Countryman* magazine.

After eighteen months at the beginning of 1942 it was becoming
plain that Blanche and I were losing our enthusiasm for writing letters
home. By then we were so involved with our American lives and family

that the one left behind seemed very remote indeed and in the callous way of children we knew Aunt Nancy was writing as regularly as she could with what we considered much greater skill than we could ever muster. My mother was plainly making a strong complaint to Aunt Nancy on the issue, whereupon we were shown this letter which had elicited a spurt of letter writing at the time. Aunt Nancy was fearful of letting the matter become a chore and was concerned that her continually nagging us to write would have the opposite effect to the one desired.

In the summer of 1943 it is still an issue between my mother and my foster mother. My mother is suggesting letters should be written at school and she received this reply.

> *I showed the girls your letter about their writing. I am puzzled and sad about the situation, although it is quite understandable. The gap is becoming too wide. I'm not sure that school exercises, which would be almost punishments, are a good basis for a happy and natural interchange of thoughts. I know that required jobs are good discipline and the children have plenty; or at least a fair share of such, both at home and at school. Neither our home or our school being completely "Progressive". The thing on which both Dick and I put great emphasis is in trying to help the individual to develop in character as well as in intellect.*

She then goes on to explain the difficulties and asks my mother to be patient. A week or so later she follows with these remarks: *I know I have failed about their writing. With Lou I think it is more than likely that doing it makes her homesick. When I speak to her about it she is more than likely to cry. With Blanche I fear it is what I call her "fecklessness".* When this was said Blanche was nearly fourteen and showing all the signs of being a typical American teenager. Later when Blanche was at boarding school in America she wrote every week because writing home was part of the timetable.

It was in the autumn of 1942 two years after our arrival that the letters have any mention of homesickness. Then Aunt Nancy writes:

> *A strange and interesting and perhaps sad thing is happening. Louise is begin-*

ning to be a bit homesick. Dick is glad because he has felt they have been too feckless about home. I don't think it is that. It seems to me that they put all their love of home and you in a very precious box and have almost consciously put it carefully away where they won't see it so often that it would make them unhappy and dissatisfied here.

Now, as Louise gets bigger she is sleeping alone in Becca's room while Becca is away at College and sometimes at night she takes a look in the corner where she keeps you and then I hear her crying and I go up and have a cheery chat sitting on the edge of her bed. The children are fond of us and entirely affectionately accept our jurisdiction but they do not love us. That is kept entirely for you which is as it should be. Only, I sometimes feel that if I could reach down a little deeper into their hearts I could help them grow more easily. However, I don't think they are unhappy at all. They laugh and sing and work and play, and eat like the most well adjusted children in the world and I think they are really happy. I know they love school and they are making lovely friends.

They are never demonstrative, but they feel sad if I don't go up at night for a goodnight kiss and to tuck them in. I don't have them say their prayers out loud this year, it was getting too racy and thoughtless, so I have told them they are big enough to have a variety of things to bring to the Almighty in private and I just remind them when I kiss them goodnight.

There is no mention of my sister showing signs of homesickness.

This letter epitomises the problem Aunt Nancy had with my mother in explaining that though we were very happy we were still her children. Saying 'we did not love' the Woods was fulfilling this purpose because we most certainly did. The homesickness was soon forgotten though there were rare occurrences later on when in one of my by now rare letters in the Spring of 1944 I write: *You are lucky to be having spring; here the snowdrops are just blooming. I always get sort of homesick around now for wild primroses and hedges. I even get lonesome for stinging nettles. We have poison ivy and it lasts for days* (as I had learnt to my cost over the years) *and you have to put calamine lotion on it. Calamine lotion is just a pink sort of thing that's watery. You can't just spit on a dock leaf to make it well. We don't even have wild bluebells or daffodils, the violets aren't half as good.* The beauti-

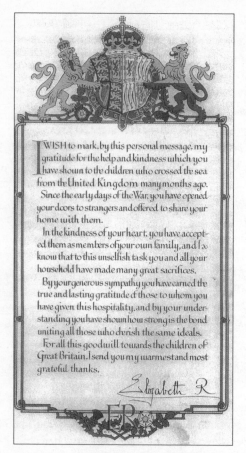

I WISH to mark, by this personal message, my gratitude for the help and kindness which you have shown to the children who crossed the sea from the United Kingdom many months ago.

Since the early days of the War, you have opened your doors to strangers and offered to share your home with them.

In the kindness of your heart, you have accepted them as members of your own family, and I know that to this unselfish task you and all your household have made many great sacrifices.

By your generous sympathy you have earned the true and lasting gratitude of those to whom you have given this hospitality, and by your understanding you have shown how strong is the bond uniting all those who cherish the same ideals.

For all this goodwill towards the children of Great Britain, I send you my warmest and most grateful thanks.

Elizabeth R

ful pale yellow primroses that cover swathes of Devon hedges in the spring filling the air with their delicate scent have always been a favourite; likewise, the Devon wild violets with their sweet scent which could be found on shady banks.

One notable letter that had arrived in Moorestown in January 1944 was one from the Queen Elizabeth of England, later the Queen Mother, expressing her appreciation to American families with English children staying with them. It was a beautifully worded and exquisitely executed illuminated sheet. Aunt Nancy comments that: *We do appreciate the gracious thoughtfulness which prompted it. I am now mentally planning to bring to her attention the problems facing parents who will have re-adjustments to worry about later and urge the sending of mothers to us when and where possible to help interpret us to you.* I have no way of knowing if such a letter was sent but it shows how aware our American family was of the changes to be faced on returning to England. By then she was pressing my mother to do just this and come and see our American home.

CHAPTER TWENTY

School and sport

Moorestown Friends School which all the children in the family attended was founded in 1785. It was not a big school, 320 pupils spread between the Elementary School, Junior High School and High School, but with a high teacher/pupil ratio. It was of a good academic standard as evidenced by Becca and Anne's success in scholarships to Bryn Mawr, one of the top flight colleges in the United States. The guiding principles of the school were based on Quaker philosophy and religious beliefs, which meant that when we had Scripture on the timetable it would be studied from a Quaker point of view. The 'Aims of the School' are set out in the paragraph below.

To train each child in good habits of study, independent thinking and in the effective use of acquired facts, skills and abilities; to create in each child the desire and ability to participate in constructive social living; to cultivate in each child an enlarging interest in the arts and sciences so that he may be able to develop further his appreciation and interpretation of Life and his contribution to it; to challenge each child to discover the Infinite within himself thereby enabling him to build an increasingly satisfying philosophy of life.

Though Quakers were probably outnumbered within the school, they were of sufficient numbers to mean that the ethos of the school was maintained. There was a very close relationship between home and school. On the evidence of the letters school staff were asked to the house at 272 West Main Street for meals or even someone's birthday party. On one occasion all the women staff were asked in for a roast lamb supper though I believe Richard and I at any rate were not included in this grown up event for I have no recollection of this episode.

School was certainly more relaxed than we had experienced back in England. No school uniform was required and relationships with staff were non-threatening. I can never remember getting into trouble at this stage in the way I did in the English School I attended when I got home again where I had a way of ending up outside the Headmistress's Office to receive a talking to for some misdemeanour. Certainly we had homework to do and there must have been sanctions when it did not appear. This is evidenced by the following episode quoted from the end of the school year *1942*.

> *During the last two days of school Lou faced grave disaster: having known all year that she must read and write reviews of 15 books during the year. Now the year was over and she had only done 12. She tried tears and tantrums all to no avail and finally got down to work and finished them up in short order. She had nearly finished a really solid book so she dashed at it and soon had it done. She remembered one she had read and not written about and she hunted out a quick and easy one at the library and covered it quickly. It was a very useful lesson, especially as much more reading will be expected of them next year when they move up to the splendid thorough Miss Swan who started Blanche off last year when she first arrived.*

Dashed is the salient word here. I was always in a hurry and always being admonished for being too slapdash.

By September 1943 Richard and I had reached 7th Grade. This was part of Junior High which meant we no longer had all our lessons with one teacher but went from room to room for each subject. The class now was so big it was divided in two and Richard and I were separated. Generally we were fairly level academically in the top half of the group, gaining similar marks, a mixture of As and Bs more of the former than the latter if things were going well. We studied English, social studies, science (mostly nature study), history, general language (an introduction to Latin and other languages) and then what Anne called the frills of music, art, gym and manual training. Richard and I had differing preferences in the subjects taught; mine were for social studies (the nearest the Americans get to geography), sciences and the frills without the music while he enjoyed the English, history and music in contrast. Sewing and making things which I enjoyed doing was mostly done at home.

At the end of this school year when I was twelve it would appear the Bs were in the ascendancy on my end of year report. The comment from Aunt Nancy is; *Lou could have done better in some subjects but I think a low mark is good for her as she is terribly cocky a good deal of the time. I think a bit of quite unprejudiced deflating is very good for what ails her.*

I have written about my adventures in botany. I was equally enthusiastic about zoology and my greatest delight was when Anne came home from College with a special present. She was having to do biology as a required science (she was a very reluctant scientist) and when their class were dissecting some dogfish they found some babies inside them. My present was a pickled baby dogfish in a jar. The rest of the family thought it was quite repulsive but I was delighted with my specimen.

While Blanche was at Westtown School during our last year in America I was able to visit her there. I wrote home in glowing terms:

Over the weekend I stayed at Westtown with Blanche. Aunt Nancy and Uncle Dick stayed with Anna Brown, the mother of Caroline Howe. (Anna Brown had written a helpful letter to my parents soon after our arrival describing the Wood family in detail so they could picture where we were. Caroline was married to my mother's cousin Ronald Howe.)

On Saturday night we had a program at Westtown. Daddy you would have loved it; about erosion. First they had the amount land wasted on a hill at a 10 degree angle, then a twenty degree angle. Third was the erosion in a forest where they have the leaves on the ground: fourth sand; fifth land with straw sort of stuff on top and pasture. The contrast was wonderful. Also they had a geyser, man-made, which they demonstrated. They had something on color blindness too.

My lifetime interest in landscape is becoming established.

Besides academic study we had all sorts of other activities such as shows and plays and probably music too. Sadly, I had no talent in these activities. Richard could perform on his banjo successfully and Blanche and Anne each had parts in plays where they acquitted themselves well. There was one occasion where I was on stage but this was in *The Nutcracker* and my role was to do handstands and cartwheels which luckily required no acting talent at all.

For my sister and me one of the best aspects of school was the organised sport. This was particularly so for Blanche who struggled in lessons but excelled in sport. A lot of letter space is devoted to Blanche's battles with Latin. It was deemed essential to one's education in those days and for the Woods with an academic outlook and two very academic daughters one of whom would become a Latin teacher, this was a new situation. I wonder she wasn' t relieved of the agony to concentrate on other subjects. It has taken fifty years for Latin to slip down the list of essential subjects taught in schools.

`The organised games were field hockey and basketball. It was voluntary to stay and play after school which usually meant we stayed. Our letters are full of our exploits and which team we were playing for.

Impromptu hockey team. Louise third from left in the back row

On one occasion when I was in 8th grade I played substitute for a Senior team because they were short of players.

"Lou, I want you to play for the Second Team on Friday." my games mistress said "Oh, oh, yes please. You really want me to play?" I asked.

"I want you to play goal." she replied. By now I was wondering if this was such a good idea after all.

"But I've never ever played in goal, Mrs McCone. I'm not sure I can."

"Come out at lunch time and I'll give you a few lessons. All you have to do is watch the ball and you're good at that." she said. So I was dressed up in all the pads and I had a very short practice and was torn between the honour of being chosen and the daunting nature of the task being asked of me.

The afternoon came and I was dressed up all over again. Being so small it was a wonder I could be seen behind the protective layers. Well, I did my best and Richard came and stood by the goal mouth in support but sadly I let in two goals and our team lost. I was devastated.

"I don't think I'll ever play in goal again". I said.

Blanche being tall and athletic played a wing forward where speed was important. By the time Blanche was at Westtown she was good enough to play in the Junior Varsity Team which was good for a 10th grader. Blanche was able to make the basketball teams successfully too. I was disadvantaged by my height, though to some extent speed could compensate for my small size. Meanwhile Richard was learning to play a good game of soccer, football to the English. Surprisingly American football was not played at Moorestown Friends as it is elsewhere in America..

CHAPTER TWENTY-ONE

Family life

When we arrived into the Wood family, Richard was the youngest with a gap of 5 years between him and Anne, the next eldest, and 7 years between him and Becca. Strangely the family configuration mirrored the pattern in my own family. Two older girls followed by a 5½ year gap then the only son. Richard's position altered with our arrival, he now became a boy among four girls, whereas my own brother with us gone, became even more precious than he was before.

Richard and I, the same age bar three months, became firm friends but also to some extent competitors. I, being the tom boy that I was, took naturally to having a boy as a playmate. Richard was quieter and more contemplative than I was; in contrast, I was quick, slapdash and untidy. We used to wrestle like puppies when we were young and honours were about even. Richard now recollects that I won our tussles but I would have said he did which suggests it was an even match. He tells me it didn't worry him any at the time. He was easy going whilst I was more competitive, I am sure there was no animosity between us.

Uncle Dick made sure that there were times when Richard, as the only boy, got his sole attention which the rest of us accepted without rancour, knowing it was his due. For instance on one occasion he took Richard fishing with Grandfather Wood on an all male expedition. There is no doubt he would have had a larger share of individual attention had we not been there. Later, I know Aunt Nancy emphasised to my mother the sacrifices that had been thrust on Richard by our presence. On the other hand we may have saved him from being overly spoiled and precious.

To illustrate his special relationship with his father there were times when Uncle Dick, just in from his day at the office, might find something around the house not quite to his liking and he would say in a stern voice, "Who is responsible for this state of affairs?" If in reply Aunt Nancy should say, "It was Richard, dear," nothing more would be said. On the other hand, if it was one of the girls then we would be suit-

Family group in the garden.
Left to right: Aunt Nancy, Louise, Becca, Richard and Uncle Dick

ably scolded. Girls at this time learnt to recognise how life was not always a level playing field.

I was a little in awe of Uncle Dick and felt him to be remote from me. Partly I think because he used long words and long sentences and there were times when I was not quite sure when he was pulling my leg or being serious. He enjoyed nothing more than having intellectual discussions with the two older girls though when we got a bit older and joined the adult supper we would listen to these conversations and no doubt learnt something from them. Even so, Blanche found them awfully boring.

Uncle Dick would leave early in the morning having breakfasted before we did and no one was allowed to disturb his morning paper at this time of day. He would not arrive back from his office until about 7 o'clock this time with the evening paper, *The Philadelphia Evening Bulletin.* Richard and I would race to get the Funnies from the back of this paper as soon as he returned. The Funnies were the comic strips in the back giving a daily story of such characters as Li'l Abner, Popeye and Little Lulu. Often Richard would go down to the station to meet the train so he could enjoy the walk home with his father. I might sometimes join them but not often.

Richard did get male companionship from his friendship with his cousin Reddie Engle who lived only six miles away at Haddonfield. Reddie, just a little older, gave him a chance to regain the balance from his female family. He would often go and stay with him or Reddie would come to 272 when there would be opportunities to enjoy boys' pastimes.

It transpired while we were in America that Reddie's father, also named Redman Engle, had met my Uncle Rendel, Mother's other brother, and had been camping with him in the Yorkshire Dales before the War, though how this had come about I do not know. Such is the Quaker network.

My sister's situation was somewhat different because she now became the middle child of the larger family. Though she played with us two younger ones at times, generally she developed her own play-mates. In particular there was Patsy Perkins from next door and Shona Edgar, the daughter of English parents living in Moorestown while her father a pilot in the R.A.F. was ferrying supplies across the Atlantic. Blanche and Shona were both pleased to find an English friend while Patsy would spend as much time at our house as she did at home and was referred to on occasions as "the ever present Patsy". Blanche and Anne were close too and once Becca went to college it was Anne who took on the role of elder sister to us all.

If there was conflict within the family it was most regularly my sister and I squabbling. We are very different personalities. I used to tease Blanche at every opportunity and was probably encouraged because I could be guaranteed to get a "rise". Blanche when she went to bed would have an array of "necessities" on the table by her bed, torch, Vaseline, handkerchief, glass of water, nose inhaler all neatly set out for any night time emergency all in the correct placings, almost like an old lady.

"Good night, girls." Aunt Nancy would say; "Time to settle down now," and she would retire downstairs for a quiet evening of knitting.

After she had gone Blanche would whisper, "Oh dear, I must just go to the John again." and off she would trot to the bathroom.

While she was gone I could quickly nip out of bed and hide her array of necessities and get back to bed and pretend to be asleep.

Back she would come. "Where are my things, Lou? What have you done with them? You've hidden them! Where are they?"

She would come and jump on me with lots of noise. An adult, usually Anne, would rapidly arrive from downstairs to find the source of trouble. Not difficult to know the culprit who would then be banished to another room at least until adult bedtime.

Our very worst fight was after Christmas in 1944. This particular episode is well remembered by all members of the family as an epic. At this time I was sleeping on my own in what in the beginning had been called the "Nursery" while Blanche was away at boarding school and I was doubtless not quite so pleased to have her back in this domain after our initial joyful reunion. Always one of our reasons for quarrelling was what was described as Blanche's extreme devotion to neatness and my terrible untidiness. I had a way of leaving a trail of mess behind me wherever I had been in the house. I enjoyed making things with my hands, craftwork and sewing in particular, so frequently I would leave a trail of magazines, rolls of cotton, half made oddments, spools of thread and goodness knows what behind me. It also meant that when Blanche was away I had a liberty to live in a muddle in our bedroom.

In this incident I upset some books she had just tidied. No, I didn't just upset them, I swept them on to the floor. As Blanche liked things to be tidy I knew anything I did to interfere with this was bound to cause ructions. Ructions there certainly were! I think it would be true to say that the reaction this time was spectacular and Blanche was hysterical with fury. A mammoth shouting match followed.

I in turn was very severely scolded. "What does thy conscience tell thee when thee behaves like this, Lou?" Quarrelling was considered a self indulgence without regard to the rest of the family. The first solution was to be sent to bed as fights were also deemed the result of tiredness and it gave the protagonists time to reflect on their behaviour. The further punishment was that instead of being banished to another bedroom I was banished to Grandmother's house with strict instructions that I was not to be allowed to visit my beloved Uncle Charlie, who lived next door, while I was staying there.

Later when things were tense again between us I went gladly to Uncle Charlie and Aunt Anna's before things got out of hand. It is difficult to explain why we had these upsets because today we are the best of friends.

I felt no resentment when I was reprimanded for my misbehaviour, knowing it was deserved and accepting my lectures and punishments as required. We benefited from the fair and liberal regime implemented by the Woods. It is evident that Aunt Nancy had misgivings about the kind of authority my mother might employ when we went home to England as shown by a letter from Aunt Nancy in January 1945.

> *"I was very much troubled by the last letter I had from you. You spoke as though you thought Blanche's enjoyment of the social side of life were something she should perhaps be ashamed of. It is true that they occupy a good deal if her mind, but we must remember that fun is a normal part of life, especially when one is 15 years old, attractive and athletic. She is not a student, I fear we can never make her into one, but she is responsible loyal in her friendships and cooperative. When one talks to her in a group she seems feckless, but if you have a real concern for her and discuss it with her in private she is understanding and wants to do the right thing. The thing we must remember is that she is no longer a child; and yet she still has childish phases 'standing with reluctant feet'. Now we discuss things with her as with another grown up".*

My mother must have voiced her unhappiness about the discipline we were receiving using as her excuse for her approach her own "Victorian upbringing" to which Aunt Nancy replied that she too had had such an upbringing as well and from an English governess at that. She then goes on:

> *"I think you have missed a great deal by not having your children to grow up with because it means you have not had touch with early adolescent people during these years and they have grown through stages you will have to bridge in imagination.*
>
> *Fundamentally they are the same as your English children, the Americanisms will soon drop off if you can ignore them. Remember they are not **Wrong** only **different**. As children dislike being different from their fellows they will be ultra English in a few months."*

CHAPTER TWENTY-TWO

Clothes

A RECURRING THEME in the letters is Aunt Nancy's concern to keep all her girls suitably dressed. Both she and my mother made clothes for us and they both seemed to consider it undesirable to buy things ready made for reasons not only of cost, though of course this was important, but also some underlying reluctance. Perhaps this was due to their Quakerism in some way. Buying ready made clothes was viewed in the same way that ready made meals are today; indicative of some sort of laziness. I find this hard to explain.

The history of Quakerism dating back to the early days was to reject the vanity of ornate clothes and to adopt simple adornment in simple colours simply sewn. The term 'Quaker grey' is still used to describe a colour of grey reminiscent of clothes worn by Quakers in times past. Additionally, it was war time and therefore necessary to economise in all aspects of life.

Both my mother and Aunt Nancy appeared to be clothes conscious to some extent and knew which colours best suited them. In answer to a query from my mother Aunt Nancy replies; *"You ask about my colours. How sweet of you to want to do something for me, but you mustn't think of such a thing. I usually use reds, pinks, violets and greens, dark in winter and lighter in summer."* While my mother was very much a blue person, taking the colour that matched her eyes.

They knew what the fashion of the time was and could tone it down to what they considered appropriate within this unwritten Quaker criteria. For my mother, this was a particular conflict. She was an attractive woman and enjoyed the attention that wearing a pretty dress or pretty hat could bring but at the same time felt guilty in so doing.

We had arrived in Moorestown with summer and winter clothes which had been christened our "trousseau" because it was so beautifully sewn. This was supplemented after my arrival by parcels from Tobo in an effort to help out. The insecurity of the post and the risk of high duty payments was discouraging for both parties when doing this. The added problem for my mother of not necessarily knowing the correct size meant that eventually this activity ceased.

To help with the mammoth task of sewing, a seamstress, Mrs Knuchols subsidised by Grandmother Wood, was employed to help out. She would be ensconced in the upstairs hall with the electric sewing machine and yards of material which had to be cut and sewn. The older girls were more frequently the recipients of these labours because many of their things could be passed down the line. This effort produced numbers of frocks, frequently pinafore frocks with ruffles over the shoulders and blouses with puffed sleeves underneath recalling Judy Garland in *The Wizard of Oz*.

The materials too brought memories of a distant age; percale and dimity cottons as well as seersucker which is still around today but then was considered quite a novelty. This last was a godsend because of its easy laundering, sensibly suggested by Emma. The easy use materials which require no ironing we take for granted today had yet to be developed so the no-iron characteristic of seer-sucker was much appreciated.

Buttonholes were a real bugbear in all this as they had to be done by hand and required careful attention and if each shirt required five, and there were several shirts, it could add up to fifteen at one sitting. Quite a formidable task; not many people nowadays sit down and sew buttonholes by hand.

Fewer dresses were sewn for me. I had more hand-me-downs than the others being the smallest in the family as well as getting cast offs from Ann Stokes, Dr. Emlyn Stokes' daughter, who was a year older than I and, coming from a wealthier household, was the owner of a great many clothes. One year I received fourteen frocks *in good condition and becoming* it was reported. I am amazed at the number, even today I would not expect to have a wardrobe so lavishly supplied.

However, I was included in the playsuits that were made, such as shorts and shirts to be worn at play. The main problem here was that as the years went by I would grow into first Blanche's then Anne's wardrobe, though never Becca's because I never reached her 5'10" height. There came a time when I considered I never, ever, had anything new that had been made or bought especially for me in the colour of my choice. If I did, it was a red letter day. Besides making new clothes there was a lot of letting out or taking in to make the passed on dresses and blouses fit the next recipient.

Special events often called for special outfits. Becca and later Anne were made special long white dresses for their School Commencements and for their Senior Proms special party dresses were sewn. I remember Becca's Commencement dress made of eyelet embroidered pique *in itself enough decoration* with a circular skirt that was eight and a half yards around the bottom. The dress had a fitted bodice and square neck and looked very lovely on tall Becca with her long red hair pulled back from a centre parting into plaits crossed over at the back of her neck. American School Commencements are always special occasions and the girl participants all carried little bouquets in paper lace doilies with ribbons attached while the boys were in smart suits parading to the stirring music of Elgar's *Pomp and Circumstance March*. Anne in her turn had a special dress for her Special Day.

Similarly, when they went up to college, there was a big sewing session to make sure they were equipped with a suitable wardrobe. Other events when special clothes were needed was when someone was performing in a play, dancing around the Maypole or dressing up for Hallowe'en. The story back in England, where clothes rationing was very strict, presented a very different picture. I was unaware of this until I returned to England in 1945 and experienced first hand what it meant.

All these clothes from a large family of seven generated an enormous load of washing and ironing which meant a great deal of work each week, even with the help of a washing machine. A lot of time and energy was needed to get the job finished because the washing machine was by no means automatic and had to be stood over as things were transferred for rinsing and then put through the electric wringer.

The modern machine that most helped the laundry was an ironing machine for "the flats". A list of items put through the ironing machine one week goes as follows:

Dozens of serviettes (because there had been company), 3 embroidered luncheon cloths, the 4 yard damask tablecloth, towels, tea napkins, pillow cases, all the under things, night clothes and this still left frocks, blouses and shirts to be done by hand.

The hand ironing became easier after Christmas 1942 when a new modern gift was received, an Electric Steam Iron, a new invention that meant the laundry didn't have to be sprinkled and dampened before the ironing task could begin. After that, 35 pairs of stockings had to be gone over to check for holes for mending. It took many hours to get through these domestic chores even with Emma's help.

Another important activity was the knitting of sweaters. Aunt Nancy was a prodigious knitter who could knit and read at the same time, hence when we were being read to she would also be knitting. She knitted in the continental fashion; that is holding the wool in the left hand, unlike the method used in England. By using a round needle, starting at the neck and working downwards she was able to hold off stitches for the sleeves to be picked up later and then continue to the waist producing a seamless raglan sweater in double quick time. Both my mother and I knitted this way. Once when on an English train happily knitting, I looked up and found all the women in the compartment watching me with fascination, quite amazed at how quickly it could be done though that red sweater for my brother was not done at speed at all.

CHAPTER TWENTY-THREE

Pets

PETS AND ANIMALS were very much part of the household at 272. When we arrived Woozer, a lovely affectionate black cocker spaniel with long droopy ears and appealing eyes, was a well established member of the family. She slept with Richard in his bedroom or more frequently on his bed.

When my sister and I arrived, we had been presented with a small grey kitten we called Smoky with four white paws and a pretty white front. I was delighted about this and happily took up the task of looking after her. However, the Wood family and Uncle Dick in particular, were very enthusiastic bird watchers and they were concerned for the bird life in the yard in the face of a predatory cat, particularly in the spring when the birds would be nesting. This meant that when spring came in 1941 it was agreed that Smoky should be found a new home.

To compensate my loss Uncle Dick said,

"Lou, I think thee should have another pet to care for."

"Oh, yes, please."

"Well, what would thee like?" asked Puddy, "How about a rabbit?"

"I think I would like a monkey." I announced

"Wouldn't thee like a parrot?" Richard suggested.

Everyone had a different idea on what the new pet should be. Unsurprisingly the monkey and the parrot were vetoed. After a lot of discussion it was decided and agreed by all that it should be a canary.

So Richard, Blanche and I were taken on an expedition to a Philadelphia pet shop to choose a canary. A sweet little yellow canary was bought with the prospect of a mate to join him later in hopes that they would set up a family in due course. They were christened Peter Pan and Wendy and soon replaced the place in my heart left by Smoky. The idea was that they should also entertain us with their trilling song. I'm not sure that that ever became a notable event even though Peter twittered companionably where he lived in his cage hanging in the dining room.

The nearest I ever got to having a monkey was when I was given the small soft toy called Chatter who I could cuddle and take to bed with me.

Woozer, the family black cocker spaniel, was loved by all the family and delighted us all by producing a litter of puppies. It was when Richard and I were in the beginning of 5th grade that Woozer had been introduced to the father, a beautiful red-gold cocker spaniel called Taffy. The expected date was the end of November around Thanksgiving time, an important date in the American calendar, also a time when school was out for a long weekend. In the meantime it was considered a good opportunity to enlighten us on the facts of life. Though I am not sure I got all the questions of reproduction sorted out at that time, it certainly helped.

Thanksgiving Feast is always on a Thursday and this time it was to be at 272 when twenty members of the family would sit down for lunch. It was on the Wednesday, the day before, that this momentous event occurred as Aunt Nancy writes. *The puppies had been busily arriving from 10.00 o'clock on. Prior to that poor Woozer had been in a very sad state with a variety of accidents every little while. So I spent the morning torn between stuffing two 17½ pound turkeys and mopping up after Woozer. There had been six accidents when I heard a crying noise and hunted all about upstairs to find her, but to no avail. I then found her in my big Queen Anne chair in the living room with a golden puppy beside her. I finally got her upstairs to bed safely, scrubbed the chair and returned to my preparations.*

Oh, the joy when we got home from school! Woozer and her family took up residence with plenty of newspapers on the floor in Richard's room while he joined us to sleep in our room. For the next few weeks we vied with each other to give the family suitable names and played with them endlessly. One lovely one called Pandora was kept and became known as Dora.

Names given to our pets were very important and often veered from the classical to the mundane. Never more so than the names we gave the chickens.

The keeping of chickens began in 1942 when we three younger ones were all given little day-old chicks at Easter. Little round chirping balls of fluff arrived to the accompaniment of our Easter Eggs and lots of excitement. They soon grew and had to be let out, fed and watered each day before we went to school. The ration they received had the glorious name of "Lay or Bust". Of course, we just were dying to know what would happen if they didn't lay and did bust.

The next Easter, 1943, these were supplemented by more baby chicks for each of the three of us. Unfortunately, mine named Pip and Pop, died soon after and were duly buried in the garden with appropriate pomp and ceremony. As compensation three more were purchased for each of us and these were given carefully chosen names. Richard's were called Bach, Gilbert and Sullivan, Blanche's Pesky, Pokey and Porky and mine Romeo, Juliet and Desdemona. Later Romeo astounded us by laying eggs. Gilbert went on to become a very handsome black and white spotted cock with a very fine red comb. He became ruler of the chicken run and at times was so fierce with anyone venturing into his domain that they were frightened to enter even when on feeding duties. Years later I was quite amazed when I learnt Richard had called his eldest son Gilbert, not after his cockerel I am glad to say, but after his father-in-law.

The cocks were justly identified to be the Sunday Roast. Unlike my husband, Graham, who tells of his experience when his much loved rabbit hopefully named Dinner did not turn out to be the relished wartime meal that was expected.

It would appear I was of a much more callous nature as the following letter written in March 1944 to my Grandfather when I was twelve years old illustrates.

Dear Grandpa,

I hope you are well. I am sorry I did not write sooner. We received your package with great joy. Aunt Nancy says she will read the Vicar *of* Wakefield *to us after we finish* Westward Ho.

*Today I did the bloody (*in America this word is taken literally*) work of chopping a chicken's head off. When its head was half off it went flopping around for several yards. I got the head off finally. Richard chopped two chickens heads off while I held them. With one of them I held it while it did all its flopping.*

The letter then goes on to other topics. What my poor grandfather thought of this activity I cannot think. Our problem was that the axe we used was not unduly sharp so what agonies the chickens went through doesn't bear considering. Can you see us trying to hold these frightened cackling creatures still enough for the guillotine to fall? We were not usually given this job but on this occasion we did it in order to earn some much needed funds. Usually this task fell to Georgie.

Georgie was the odd job black man who did jobs in the yard depending on the season, tasks like chopping and stacking wood, sweeping leaves or weeding the vegetable patch. He had apparently arrived at the back door during the Depression in the 1930s asking to do a job in return for a meal and had stayed around ever since. He was a small wizened little man with an accent I found difficult to understand and hair growing white like cotton wool which I found quite fascinating. He wore his jacket done up with a large safety pin and worked part time for us in a rather haphazard way. He would not have been old enough to have been a slave but I imagine his parents were. When not working he might be found in a rocking chair on the back porch or in a corner of the kitchen gossiping with the faithful Emma.

On one occasion Georgie was down in the cellar clearing up. The cellar had a natural propensity to becoming a junk store as is the way with these places. It housed the boiler for the heating which demanded a constant supply of solid fuel, especially in winter, as well as housing Aunt Nancy's preserves, our sleds out of season and other such bits and pieces.

On this occasion it was housing Richard's pet grass snake in a glass tank. Suddenly, there was a mighty crash and Georgie appeared hot foot at the top of the cellar steps wide eyed and horrified. He was absolutely terrified of snakes. No one had thought to warn him of this harmless creature lurking down there. Not until the snake had been captured and removed was he prepared to finish his work. Later Aunt Nancy took him to the Zoo to see the snakes there but I have no memory of whether this helped or hindered the problem.

When Richard and I were discussing the animals one day we decided that really Blanche should have a pet to call her own other than the chicks she had had at Easter.

"Why don't we get her a rabbit?" Richard suggested.

"Yeah, that's a swell idea." I replied. "How can we pay for it?" I wondered. "How much money have you got?"

We added up our savings but there wasn't enough. The only answer was to do some chores to get some extra finance as well as persuading Uncle Dick to make a contribution. That way we could do it.

We bought her a beautiful big soft grey chinchilla rabbit which was duly named Benjamin. Blanche was delighted, particularly as it was a complete unbirthday surprise present. Later in the year, on her real twelfth birthday, we had another surprise for her when Richard and I bought Benjamin a wife. In great secrecy we had gone to the farm to buy the doe and kept her hidden in the unused fireplace in Becca's room where I was sleeping, until the next day, when she was presented at the birthday supper in a large cardboard box wrapped in brown paper with lots of travel labels made for the outside. Benjamin's new wife was called Flopsy

Then, when Richard and I were around eleven years old, we decided to go in for goat keeping. Blanche was a little less enthusiastic about some of these activities but would give us lots of free advice on how we should be doing it. Blanche could be free with her advice at times!

By this time Richard was becoming interested in farming and would often visit his best friend Howdy Taylor who was a farmer's son. He very much enjoyed helping around this farm and would dearly have loved a cow, while I was well aware of my land based roots in Devon. In order to start this venture we had to invest $2.00 of our own money to buy the kids; equal to 15 shillings in English money at the time, which was quite a big outlay. I quote from my letter home dated May 1943.

"Guess What? I don't suppose you'll be able to, but I HAVE A GOAT. Richard has one too. His is black and white and mine is white. We have to feed them from bottles and it is very difficult because they won't suck properly, especially mine. We haven't named them yet. I asked Aunt Nancy to ask Anne to try and think up some names because she is not doing anything but lying in bed all day in hospital for she had her appendix out on Monday. The poor thing shall miss her exams and have to take them later on when she is better. We built the house which they live in from some glass crate boxes which we bought instead of new lumber which would have cost more.

The black and white billy goat was named Roger and the white nanny, Heidi. They were really cute. Cute was a word I greatly over used at that time though in this case I think it fairly described these cuddly looking little animals that played and gambolled in their pen in the back yard.

At one time Richard and I had tried to make a goat cart but like many of our grand ideas it proved unrealistic. The goats only lasted until the next spring by which time they were no longer the cute little kids we started with but growing into adult goats with a voracious appetite that was having a deleterious effect on Aunt Nancy's precious spring garden flowers. Added to this was the problem of Roger the billy goat, who had

The goats Roger and Heidi

an increasingly unpleasant smell, though I do not think that could have bothered me because the next thing I was asking for was a skunk. One of those seemingly attractive small black animals with a white stripe down its back and a big bushy tail that also looked cute when young.

However, it has a nasty habit of excreting an extremely noxious spray over anything it feels threatened by. To be treated thus by a skunk usually involved putting every stitch of clothing you were wearing when attacked on to a bonfire.

"Well if I can't have a skunk of my very own, what can I have?" I asked.

"What I really, really want is a collie dog like Lassie in the film *Lassie Come Home*".

Like such requests, no notice was taken for a long time but I must have been unbearably persistent on this occasion because eventually the following August my dearest wish was granted when I was given not exactly a collie but a crossbred collie type puppy collected from the dog pound. It was by way of a very early birthday cum Christmas present, and was the most beautiful tawny coloured little puppy I could have wished for. One of the many regrets on returning to England was having to leave Sherry behind.

CHAPTER TWENTY-FOUR

Money

I T WAS THE CONCERN of my parents that our arrival would not put too great a strain on the Woods' finances. One of the early and rare letters from Uncle Dick to my father appreciates this concern and points out that fortunately the fees for Moorestown Friends School, which was a private school, were covered by a liberal scholarship from Friends. In 1944 this amounted to $250 a year for a 7th Grader. I have already mentioned that my visit to summer camp was covered by subsidies from local Friends. Early on, in answer to questions about costs, Aunt Nancy, tongue in cheek, was wondering if they would actually make a profit on our stay because of all the help they were getting from the Meeting. This position gradually changed as time went on as I shall explain.

There is no doubt that my father arranged for as much money as was allowed by the currency regulations of the time to be sent to help cover the cost of our upkeep. In later years my mother complained that this had not been acknowledged by the Woods but the letters belie this. I believe Uncle Dick was assuming every cheque was receipted by the bank which was not the case, but even so, they expressed their gratitude for the help this supplement provided on many occasions as illustrated in a letter of 27th February 1942 which says:

> *We do appreciate your thinking of sending the new allowances, according to the new rulings, but Dick and I do not want you to try and do it if it makes you cut yourselves too short. We know that you have been under far more rigid restrictions than we have.*

So far we have managed to get along pretty well, even with our augmented family and although we always have to plan our finances carefully we live in great comfort. Our great shortage is domestic assistance so we have never quite caught up with anything, laundry cleaning or mending. We could be much better were I a more concerned housewife.

We have much more electric domestic machinery than you do I believe, with the refrigerator, washing machine, ironing machine, sewing machine and vacuum cleaner. Of course I know you have the vacuum cleaner and sewing machine but our laundry helps are the greatest savers of time and strength, especially as our laundries have been so big.

This money continued to come; for example, in 1942 £72 was sent which was increased to £114 in 1943. Many considered the restrictions too great and questions were asked in the House of Commons in January 1942, requesting the Chancellor of the Exchequer to relax the restrictions. By June 1944 when plans were being made to send Blanche to the Quaker boarding school at Westtown on the other side of Philadelphia it was decided that the money sent by my father would be put towards the fees. The school fees amounted to $700 a year, $350 coming from a scholarship the school would give her and the rest covered by money sent from England, which gives some idea of the amount of money my father was sending. This was equivalent to £130 then but more like ten times that in today's money. Blanche maintains the Lintons, the family we didn't go to, paid her Westtown fees; my guess is they paid the Friends' Scholarship part.

My father would have been able to afford these contributions reasonably well at this time although not rich my parents were comfortably off. The Vineries had 7 acres of glasshouses and 70 acres of land around, the former grew tomatoes and the latter was pasture and cereals. Dodovens with the apple orchards was also about 70 acres which, besides the apple trees, had a house cow and followers. These enterprises employed 50 workers making them one of the larger employers in the village of Elburton at this time. My grandfather as well as setting up the Vineries also had a tool and hardware shop in Plymouth, a small independent business providing essential equipment for home and business.

The shortage of money in the Wood household is illustrated by the importance attached to the need for Becca to gain a Scholarship to attend Bryn Mawr College when she left school. It was not an unrealistic wish as she graduated top of her class "Cum Laude" and passed the College Boards with flying colours and thereby received $500 a year for four years. This was enough to pay half her college expenses for the four years of study. Anne in her turn proved just as academically able as her sister and won a Scholarship as well. She had come top in three of her college entrance exams as well as receiving the Phi Beta Kappa award at her school Commencement.

Bryn Mawr, as well as being one of the top women's college in the country had the added advantage of being run by Friends. It was endowed by Friends and the Trustees and Board of Managers were all Friends at that time. However, there were other costs associated with going to College such as having to provide the soft furnishings for your room and new clothes, mostly home made as well to save costs.

In a letter dated March 1941 there is a reference to the rise in living costs by about 14%. This was put down by Aunt Nancy to the gradual increase in the cost of meat and clothing and some fresh vegetables such as lettuce, string beans, spinach and carrots. These latter would have been shipped up from Southern states like Florida where there is all year round sunshine. At that time New Jersey grew a lot of fruit and vegetables but things were only available in the appropriate season. Today we think nothing of having items like tomatoes on the supermarket shelves all the year round but at that time the movement of fresh produce in refrigerated railway wagons was only in its infancy. Meanwhile, vegetables grown in the garden in summer could be relied on. Beans, corn on the cob and tomatoes (grown outdoors) all helped augment the food bill.

It was later in the summer of 1943 that the concern for money became more acute as Uncle Dick had to take a reduction in salary. This meant that pressures on the family budget became more and more severe. For instance, letters now were sent surface mail more frequently and not by the luxury of air mail.

Grandmother Wood *like the sweet soul that she is* helped with a lot of costs, especially for the English contingent. She paid for Emma, the help, mine and Blanche's clothes and shoes as well as Blanche's and my orthodontic tooth straightening. Grandmother's Christmas and birthday presents often took the form of some item of clothing such as a red snow suit I received on one occasion, that had been bought especially for me and was not a hand me down..

Grandfather Wood was Chairman of the Board of the Esterbrook Fountain Pen Company so Grandmother was well able to subsidise their eldest son and family in this way. Aunt Nancy's side of the family by then was not so well placed. Misfortune had befallen them years previously with the disappearance of her grandfather's estate left in trust with an ancient friend and lawyer who proved not to be as trusty as his friends and clients thought.

Another bonus was that generously, no bills had been preferred from the regular dentist, the oculist nor the Ear Nose and Throat specialist who took out Blanche's tonsils nor the regular doctor, Cousin Emlen, who was a close cousin of Uncle Dick's. In fact Cousin Emlen's youngest daughter was the source of many of the successful hand-me-down dresses I wore.

Occasionally "extras" could cause alarm and yet somehow a way could be found to pay for them. When Blanche started her year at Westtown Boarding School she longed for proper ice skates and was bought a beautiful pair of white booted figure skates at the vast sum of $11.85 and a shoe ration stamp as well. This was considered really extravagant and, like other extravagances, would be identified as a birthday or Christmas present.

The Quaker approach to money was that wealth and the pursuit of wealth should not be an end in itself. Money should be used to provide a standard of living to get through life comfortably and one should be content with this. It was the tradition to live simply without high extravagances, for instances parties were very much homespun affairs not costing a lot of money. It did not mean life need be unhappy, it certainly was not, but we learnt , or tried to, not to be envious of others more prosperous than ourselves.

It was the very honest approach to money in the 19th century that

led to Quaker businesses becoming successful. They also gained a repu-
tation for caring for their workers. As an example, it was their tradition
to ask the correct price for an item of goods rather than bargain, considering it more truthful to name the true value of a product.

We children appreciated our financial situation so learnt to save our
pocket money for birthday and Christmas presents as well as making
presents in order to stretch the money further. The alternative was to
try and earn money for particular projects when the need arose. Jobs
like cleaning windows or extra gardening could be a source of extra
funds.   It was cleaning the hairdresser's windows that enabled my
friend Dorothy Porter and me to have enough funds to hire a tandem
for a special bicycle ride we had been longing to take.

I do not think it was shortage of money that drove the 'gang' to
stage a robbery, however. It was Richard's idea.

"I know; we'll rob the Five and Ten Store," he announced. It was
decided and sure enough we did. The Five and Ten was not a big store
in Moorestown, the equivalent of Woolworths selling the cheapest
merchandise in town. I think the gang in this instance were Richard's
pals Charlie Robinson and Billy Leconey. Charlie, Billy and I but not
Richard went into the store at once and wandered around looking at
the displays of goods laid out on the counters. While one of us would
make a legitimate purchase, the rest quietly shoplifted items we fancied
which we slipped into our pockets, hoping the bulges did not show.

Amazingly we were not found out which made the adventure more
exciting. When we did this, for some reason Richard was at home sick
in bed so though it was his grand scheme he did not join the shoplift-
ing spree. Instead we brought our ill gotten gains back for him to
inspect. We displayed our loot on his bed.

"Look, I got all these pencils and erasers. It was really easy." I pro-
claimed.

"Yeah" said Charlie, "but I thought Billy was going to get caught
when that other lady came in the store."

If one was not blessed with a conscience it was possible to see how easy it
was to take up a "Life of Crime". But our solid Quaker upbringing had made
sure we did have a conscience with the result that our misdemeanour

preyed on our minds. I think it was Richard who finally confessed; he after all had dreamt up the whole plot and put the rest of us into the "firing" line so had reason to be doubly guilty. The outcome was that we received a severe "bawling out", were marched back to the store to return the stolen goods, confess our sin and receive another dressing down from the manager plus the inevitable;

"Lou, does thy conscience not tell thee this is not the way to behave?"

CHAPTER TWENTY-FIVE

The James family

M Y SECOND AMERICAN SUMMER was spent with the James family who lived on the other side of Philadelphia at Wallingford, Pennsylvania. My sister and I had met Mary and Caroline James at summer camp the previous year and had visited them during the 1941 Christmas vacation, very successfully so we had been asked again this time to join the family for a vacation in the summer of 1942. The Jameses were known to the Woods as Aunt Dottie James as a class mate of Aunt Nancy's younger sister at Westtown School where Blanche was to go later, as well as being the younger sister of one of her own closest girlhood friends. Uncle Bob James, a businessman in Philadelphia like the Woods was very involved with Quaker activities and was Treasurer of the main Philadelphia Peace Committee.

Before embarking on this vacation, the James girls had been to stay with us at Moorestown for a few days when we had enjoyed a trip to the zoo and an all day picnic by a lake with lots of swimming. There is a letter from Aunt Dotty written with great sensitivity describing our stay, which included a trip to the Pocono Mountains in the Appalachians. To look at, she was slightly plump with curled dark hair and glasses and a gentle sense of humour. Like Aunt Nancy she was a sensible tolerant mother with whom I remember accepting with no qualms. She was easy to talk to and I could discuss with her matters of childhood angst quite happily; perhaps her nurse's training made this so. She had a German refugee called Magda who helped her look after her children. Besides Mary and Caroline, there were Peggy and Johnny who were younger than Caroline so that made six of us when we were there.

Her letter follows.

> Pocono Lake Preserve
> Pennsylvania
> August 2nd 1942

Dear Lawsons,

It is six weeks ago yesterday that your two girls came to us for the summer and to say that I am chagrined that all this time has gone without my writing you is to put it very mildly indeed.

We came yesterday to Pocono to camp for a month in the woods and to live apart from telephones and all that goes with civilised existence. I have been living for these days for some time and promising myself a letter to you almost upon arrival here. At the moment all six children, accompanied by our faithful Magda, who since 1933 has been part of our household, have gone swimming. Bob, who drove up with us yesterday, has gone back to the grind and I am at least beginning this letter to you.

I could go into long ecstasies about your children and all its meaning to ours to have them as part of the family this summer but I am sure that what you want is something more specific. Perhaps Nancy Wood has already told something of the set up which exists in our household and of the nearness of the ages of yours and ours. Blanche is the oldest of the four, (12 at this time) then Mary, then Lou, then Caroline. They pair off quite naturally. I don't need to tell you how different Blanche and Lou are. When I tell you that there is just as much difference between ours as between yours and that in the four there is a little bit of everything you will have a tiny idea of why it is so much fun to have them. Being one of six myself I consider our family this summer just right. Peg and Johnnie, the two younger ones are six and four.

Nancy showed me your letter about courses of study looking ahead. I read part of it to the girls who were delighted with your prediction that Lou will doubtless wind up in the circus. Her coordination is not to be sneezed at and fearlessness added to it makes quite a combination. She is just as likely to be found standing on her head in the middle of the road as not. I came on her yesterday doing cartwheels down the road toward the place they were heading for a swim. Next she was walking on her hands in the same direction and getting there quite as fast as the rest of us. A few minutes later she and Caroline were following fast on Mary's heels and leaping into space from the high diving board. By today doubtless Blanche will be following suit but I'm thankful she is cautious when not sure. Four daredevils might be one too many. Nancy tells me they didn't either of them swim when they came to these parts. I only wish you could see them now. Although Blanche is less daring than Lou she is no less determined and she gets there with less waste of motion.

Blanche and Mary are both on the brink of leaving childhood and while not in the least sophisticated (in fact quite the reverse) there is now a definite gap between them and Lou and Caroline when it comes to choice of books and interests. I'm not meaning that this is just new but rather it is interesting to watch developments. I don't know how much Nancy has talked with Blanche about growing up. I have recently come upon a book recommended by our Yearly Meeting's Marriage Council called "Mothers and Daughters" If the right moment comes I want to read it with the two older ones. It is well done by an experienced person and the kind of thing I would have loved to have when I was about their ages. If it proves to be a good thing to do and unless I find that plenty has already been done on behalf of Blanche I will try to send you a copy so you will know just what it contains. I think nothing has made me suffer vicariously on your behalf as much as trying to realise what it would be like to have Mary away right at this crucial time in her life. Perhaps it is no more so than any other time and perhaps I'm getting more emotionally involved myself as I see her growing beyond the place of almost complete dependence.

You can be thankful indeed that Blanche and Lou landed in the household Wood for they seem to feel as at home about being there as though they were in their own home. A real tribute to both the Woods and the Lawsons.

One of the things you would love about this arrangement is the spontaneous nonsense that is always coming to the fore. Of course, they have their moments of being annoyed with each other but taking it by and large they are a very congenial quartet. We had hardly arrived yesterday when Caroline and Lou set to work gathering twigs with which they erected a perfectly adorable little "cabin". It was really a work of art. We had all admired it when without warning Lou came tripping along, caught her foot on a stone, fell against the side of it and down it went, flat. They are all set to start again and who knows but what they might have learned something about foundations.

It is now Monday morning and I am more than ever convinced that this is going to be a wonderful experience for everybody concerned. The children all have their responsibilities and take turns doing beds, dishes etc. There is an atmosphere of peace and calm in these woods that make one forget what the world is like. Here's hoping being apart like this will make us better able to carry our weight when we leave this heavenly spot.

The chance to read with Blanche and Mary came sooner than I expected. While Lou and Caroline were exploring in a row boat the two older ones and I settled ourselves for one of the best times I've had with them at all. They are both keen about the book and want more. The fact that they are so uninhibited and could talk as easily as they did reassured me no end.

There are no words with which I can express the things Bob and I feel on your behalf. He has said several times; "I wonder whether our kids could take this kind of experience as the Lawson's have". Much as I admire the children and wonder the same thing, it is you parents whom I marvel. There is a quality of adaptability in children which makes such things possible for them comparatively speaking but how you have endured the separation is more than my imagination allows me to conceive.

I won't dwell on this but had to tell you that we admire you no end and are looking forward to the time when this dreadful and unholy holocaust (that isn't the way to spell that) is over and either in England or America we can meet. In the meantime please accept our sincere wishes on your behalf and know that among the good things from our point of standpoint is having your girls with us. Incidentally, I hope I can get them to do better about writing you. I fear I have been very lax about reminding them that letters are overdue.

Very sincerely,
Dorothy Biddle James

The Jameses were probably better off than the Woods. They lived in a large house built with stone and a large garden where there was plenty of room to play. However, one of the best parts of staying there for me was all the swimming we did. They did not have a swimming pool in the garden but there was one very near by to which we had unlimited access. Mary and Caroline were both excellent swimmers so we learnt a lot from them besides having plenty of opportunity to practice. A letter written by me with illustrations, after my return bubbles with enthusiasm for all the things we had done.

272 West Main St
Moorestown

Sept.9, 1942
Dear Mummy and Daddy,
It has been an awful long time since I wrote you last. I think it was at the beginning of the summer. Anyway I'll try and start at the beginning, At the beginning of the summer we were at the James's which I suppose you know. At there house I learnt to do many dives; I'll try and name as many as I can. First the front dive, then back dive which I learnt to do by Mary. I learnt in about three days.

I will finish tomorrow because I have to go to bed; I am sleeping by myself in Becca's room.
Sept 10

Then I can do a front flip, you do a summersault in the air and go in feet first. And a sit down dive (sit on the end of the board and go in head first) I can do a back flip but don't do them right and I hit the board, it is a back summersault in the air. I can do a back sit down dive and a "Spank the Baby", ouch, you sit on the water. I think it is fun to go to the shallow end of the pool and Caroline (the one my age) would stand with her legs apart and I would swim under them and get up so Caroline would be on my shoulders, then Caroline would do the same and so on. It is like a wheel.

In August we went to Pocono which is in the mountains of Pennsylvania. (I see I crossed out my efforts to try and spell Appalachians). *Up there we made a raft. It was made of four logs five feet long and five*

*inches wide. We cut the logs from fallen trees and put them together with
rope. Then we got some boards to put on top to make it flat. then when
Aunt Dotty and Caroline went home to get Uncle Bob they brought with
them some canvas cloth so we wouldn't get splinters. Then we could dive of
it at our own dock. We anchored it to a stone.*

*Another thing we did was cut firewood with a saw which uses two
people; it was great fun to work. We would take turns doing it with Uncle
Bob.*

*Another thing we did was make a hut out of sticks which I will tell
about later because I am going out to play. (Later) This hut had a fork
stick at each corner and sticks across. We had a back log fire beside it. It
also had hemlock on the floor and ferns on the roof. In the evenings we
would sing there. One night Caroline and I wanted to sleep out there and
when we had got the bed made and Caroline was fixing the pillows a stick
fell down then another and Magda was holding the hut as best she could to
stop it from falling. In the mean time I went for Uncle Bob for help.
Magda is a German girl who lives with and helps the James'. Finish
tomorrow. Uncle Bob came and made it stay up but we couldn't sleep out
there. I was taking a blanket in over my head and I bumped into a tree and
started rolling.*

*While we were there we took an overnight hike which was great fun.
We slept with our feet in a hut and our heads out. We cooked our meals by
a fire. Once Magda and I went out hunting birch bark but I didn't get to
making anything because the bark would insist on rolling up.*
Piles of love

> *Louise*

P.S. I will keep sending chapters like this till I get caught up with time.

I think the hut mentioned here was a different hut from the one that
collapsed at Wallingford. Making huts and living wild, preferably in
overalls and lumber jacket, was my idea of rapture. As Aunt Nancy and
Aunt Dotty agreed I was a natural "Bushwhacker", unlike Blanche who
had to overcome her natural aversion to spiders and other creepy
crawlies to participate.

CHAPTER TWENTY-SIX

Discipline and going to the movies

A S THE LENGTH OF TIME we were away from England increased it becomes clear that our parents were growing perturbed by the fact they were no longer able to direct the development of their daughters. It is evident from the content of the letters that one issue upsetting my mother was the frequency we went to the movies. The "Movie" debate went along similar lines to the "Television" debate that takes place today about how much and what sort of programmes are suitable for young people.

Blanche, now an American teenager or, as they were called in those days a "Bobby Soxer", took delight in reporting all the movies she had been to in her letters back home, even admitting to going twice in one day on one occasion, though this was when she had been staying with the James family who, as I have mentioned earlier, looked after us at holiday times on a fairly regular basis. Blanche and Mary knew the names of all the film stars and cut pictures of them out of magazines to put on their bedroom walls. In the same way they always listened to the "Hit Parade", just like teenagers today follow "Top of The Pops", when the most popular songs of the day would be listed in order of popularity. Singers like Frank Sinatra and Bing Crosby were often featured in the top ten.

Blanche by now was a tall, attractive, athletic and fun loving girl who enjoyed the company of boys. Here is the letter from Aunt Nancy in April 1943 reporting one of her escapades.

*The great excitement here has been your daughter Blanche, who is growing
up almost too fast. She has been invited to the moving pictures by a boy in
her class. The first invitation we refused because they were going to the
James's. Last night I found a note saying the boy had called up again and
she hoped it was alright because she **was going**. I gave her early supper
and she went off happy as a lark and pretty as a picture but she must be
home by 10 o'clock. And now it is 10:30 and she is not home so you see I
am going to have my troubles.*

*The boy is a nice lad, well mannered and from a good Quaker home and
the picture is a good picture. But I cannot let this late home business go on
and I know she will resent any interference. I am a very green hand at this
sort of thing as our own girls have never had any attention from boys. Of
course, I want her to have a good time but she is pretty young and immature
to have "dates". I rather surmise I wont allow any more as she evidently
doesn't know how to say when its time to go home even though I had quite a
talk with her about it beforehand. Lou went to the same picture with some
friends and she has been home and in bed asleep for the last hour."*

The letter goes on to other news and then continues:

*Well, my dear, Blanche is indeed a gay girl. She has just come in at
11:30p.m. having been to Philadelphia, an hour away by bus having been
to one of the big city picture theatres and generally having had a very nice
time. She had told the boy she was to be home at 10 but he just didn't pay
any attention. They were to meet another youthful pair but they did not
turn up; so they went alone.*

*I tried not to spoil it for her tonight but I should never have
allowed such a grown up lark for children that age and will see that it
does not happen again. I may talk to Mrs. Hitchcock, the boy's Mother,
and will certainly go over it with Blanche again tomorrow. The mere
fact that we thought they were here at a proper young peoples picture
while they were gallivanting about like grown ups concerns me. Somehow they should have told us; and yet I can see B's embarrassment in
being punctilious.*

*I may speak to the Principal of the school for advice as I want to help
her to make wise judgments and not just seem to be against good times as*

such. Don't worry about it. The younger we are when such lessons come the sooner we have learned them and can go on to other things.

Just about two weeks later this letter is followed by another describing subsequent events.

Dear Joan,

I have felt very badly about my last letter to you having been so full of fuss about Blanche having been out so late. Dick kept telling me not to worry you with it and I was so upset myself I just poured it right out. I am sorry, please forgive me. Of course, I was worried that night and very torn about what I should do about it.

*I did not lecture her that evening because she was too tired and had really had too much fun to have it spoiled at once by a fussy grown up. But a few days later when the question of another evening expedition came up I said **NO** and we had quite a solid discussion of our policy in the matter. I explained:*

1. that she is still too young to handle difficult decisions, as was shown by the first expedition
2. that I have a great concern that the movies shall not be attended frequently, or at all, unless we know what the play is and it is not only harmless but is actually worthwhile seeing
3. that we never go on school nights
4. that we hate to seem strict or unreasonable: but these rules stand
5. that we know young people want to have fun together and to that end they may have candy pulls or picnic suppers any Friday or Saturday evening they want them, if they will see to it that different people are asked each time and they do not become a small in-growing group. The parties not to exceed 10 in number."

The result was that a "candy-pull" was immediately considered and when David called up to invite her to the movies she immediately countered with her party idea which was accepted with joy.

They all arrived at about 8:00p.m. and played hide and seek in the dusk until we had finished in the kitchen and had measured out the kettles of molasses, sugar etc. They had great fun and did not make too frightfully much noise. A little after 10 o'clock we gave them ice cream and cookies and they went home thinking it all a great success. The next time they are going to come at 5 o'clock and cook their own suppers down in the garden and play outdoors and go home earlier.

This is my first experience with young things who have a great interest in boys. Our big girls entirely missed that phase due to being more intellectually minded, I guess, so I hope I may be led to handle this stage properly."

Much love,

Nancy

Becca and Anne were certainly not involved with boys at school though partners could generally be found to escort them to dances when necessary. The college they went to was women only so there was less opportunity to get involved then. Anne never married while Becca married later to someone ten years older than herself.

My sister replied in May on learning that mother was shocked to hear about her coming home from the movies at 9.30pm. (This suggests the news of the 11:30 night out hadn't yet reached her) Blanche wrote:

Aunt Nancy said that in a letter you wrote to her that you were shocked to hear that I was coming home from the movies at 9:30. Well, you just don't know your 13 year old daughter. You will have to realise that I am older than I was when I left England. I go to bed at 9.00pm. every night so 9.30pm is really not very late you know. After all in America we have fun especially our crowd. In America we go out with boys as Aunt Nancy has probably told you. We have fun. Don't get poor ideas about me please.

Blanche's letter goes on with her version of the very late night out.

*Just before spring vacation a boy, David Hitchcock, called me up to ask me to go on a date. I couldn't because I was going to the James to see Mary and Caroline. After the vacation he called me up again and I said yes. He came for me at seven and we went to Philly to see a movie, it was really good. The name of it was 'Happy Go Lucky'. We came home at 11:30 and **that is late**. Aunt Nancy gave me a bawling out and I guess I did deserve it that time as that is kind of late.*

He called me up again but Aunt Nancy would not let me go so I gave a

*molasses candy party, did we have fun. Molasses candy is cooked, then you
let it get hard and after that you pull it until it is a yellow color. The stuff
is very sticky but we didn't care. We pulled it and threw it so it stuck on the
ceiling; after we tired of pulling it we went into the dining room and had
ice cream and cake. Then we broke up; it was then 11:00. The next morning the kitchen was a sight and everything was sticky.*

The problem was now beginning to arise of getting our mother to
accept and understand aspects of our American way of life and fur-
thermore, the changes in us as we grew up away from her sight and
influence.

Later in November 1943 there is yet another letter from Aunt Nancy
in response to two from my mother and from what it says it is quite
evident that my mother is still not happy with how her daughters are
being brought up. By now we had been in Moorestown three years
Blanche was just turned fourteen and I was eleven. There had obviously been recent news of even more visits to the cinema which had
upset my mother again and she had brought Aunt Nancy to task for
allowing it.

Here is the reply my mother received.

*I make haste to set your mind at rest about Blanche and the "flicks". The
letters that upset you so much must have been written from Wallingford
(where the Jameses lived) and that terrific dose out there was adminis-
tered, according to Dorothy, in the hope they would never want to see
another, as Francis suggested. I must say I was as annoyed as you were by it
because I do not feel that they have enough discrimination yet to really be
able to tell the good from the bad and unless I know that a picture is fun-
damentally fine I prefer them not to see it. However, when the children are
there we must accept their theories of education and actually the results
soon disappear. I feel our family is very quiet and provincial and it is good
for your children to get glimpses of other Quaker groups.*

How I wish I could see the letter from my mother that generated these
explanations because this was not all, later in the same letter there are
further comments in answer to criticisms from my mother on the subject of discipline.

*I have been quite troubled in realizing that you do not think I am firm enough in my discipline; and you are quite right. My experience of forcing children makes me feel it to be less satisfactory than leading them. First because it relieves them of the burden of deciding between right and wrong which I think they need to learn early and practice constantly. Secondly because it seems to me that when "discipline is maintained" there is sometimes a feeling of unease between the discipliner and the disciplinee. My hope is to help them to discipline themselves, at adult suggestion if necessary, and to develop in themselves the power of acting because **they feel it** to be right rather than because I expect obedience. I am not sure which is the perfect system. It always seemed to me that the "obedience" school of thought has fewer headaches for parents but slower developing children, because their children accept their elders decisions and don't learn to think for themselves. While my school of thought has a few years of agony but is repaid by having capable, thoughtful dependable young people at a much earlier age. Actually where the system is tried from birth there is no agony. The hard thing for both child and parent is to switch from one school to the other in the middle.*

In reading this letter now, I can recognise from where my own views on education have sprung. As a teacher I have always felt it very important to develop self-discipline within the pupils and children in my care. To do this it is necessary to trust them to do what is right even if mistakes are made in the process. I can illustrate this from my own experience.

When I was teaching in Scotland I was horrified when I first arrived at the school where I taught to be given a tawse with which to punish the pupils. This is a hard rubber thong used to hit the outstretched upturned palm of miscreants. I would never have contemplated using corporal punishment. On one occasion when berating a pupil for misbehaviour one of the other pupils in the class chimed in, "Go on , hit him, Miss."

My response was "No, he must learn to behave properly himself – the easy way out is to have me hit him. He must learn to take responsibility for his own conduct."

CHAPTER TWENTY-SEVEN

Fires

I T WAS NOT ONLY the fathers who were involved with fire-fighting. Richard, Blanche and I also became involved, Richard most of all. Not truly as fire-fighters but very interested bystanders. The fire station was only a little way up the road from 272. The Moorestown Fire Service was voluntary, made up of men who worked in the town and could be summoned into action when the need arose. The summons was done by sirens and ringing bells and the pattern of rings would indicate which part of town the fire was. Richard early on had learned the code so he could guide us to the right part of town. As soon as we heard the bells ringing we would drop whatever we were doing and leap on our bikes and cycle off as fast as we could to watch the action. Most commonly the fires were grass fires but now and then it might be a more serious house fire.

Blanche describes it well in one of her letters in 1942.

Lately there have been grass fires. As children have holidays on Saturdays and some men also have a holiday they decide to burn the rubbish and then the fire spreads and of course if there is any field at the back the grass burns and the red fire engine goes down the street. We get on our bicycles and go after the fire engines which is fun. Yesterday this was the fourth or fifth fire and the siren went off and the men got on to the engines and we followed them. They were all looking for a grass fire and found it was a house not even finished being built. The firemen thought some kid had lit it. It did not do much harm; only burnt a cellar door and a board above it and around it. The glass in the door cracked and burnt. This meant a new door.

She tells of another grass fire on a Saturday this time one of four in one afternoon. This time it was Mrs Hillman, a next door neighbour. *Everybody was pleased as there will be violets on her hill in Spring.*

We weren't beyond doing our own grass burning as I write at the same time.

Daddy, we are trying to burn the field in back of the house for two weeks but it insists on raining. Richard is a half member of Hose Company No. 1 (or the fire house). I think we can burn the field today.

Richard gained a Junior Fireman Certificate. He spent a lot of his spare time up at the fire house "helping" the firemen. If you couldn't find him at home that would be the first place to look.

On November 1943 I write of another occasion.

I just went to a huge house fire about half a mile down the road. The whole house was up in flames and all four of Moorestown's fire engines were there. Some of the firemen were dressed up in their equipment. They had ladders up the side of the house and were fighting the flames from above. A tree was on fire too and we thought that some of the branches were going to fall on somebody but they didn't luckily. It started from a trash pile. Some of the firemen were soaked from the hoses from above.

There wasn't always a fire to watch to provide us with excitement. One day when there was nothing happening I had a fine suggestion:

"Why don't we pretend we are upstairs when there is a fire raging down below and we have to escape out the window on knotted sheets to get to the ground?"

"Lou, I don't think that's a good idea at all. It's much too dangerous," replied my sister. She was of a much more cautious nature and tried often to stem my mad cap schemes.

"What do you think, Richard?"

"Well, I don't know," he answered; "I don't think Mom would like us using her sheets."

Somehow I must have prevailed because the next thing was we were rummaging around in the depths of the cellar looking for a rope. Discretion had won on the matter of the sheets. A rope was found and tied to the leg of Blanche's bed which was near the window and dropped out to reach the ground.

Out I went as fearless as ever, negotiated the window sill and climbed down the rope.

"It's easy, you have a go, Richard." He managed the manoeuvre successfully and then it was Blanche's turn.

"Oh, I can't," she said.

So we other two did it again to show her how easy it was. Eventually we persuaded her and with much misgiving we got her on to the window sill all ready to descend and holding the rope, ready to climb down. At that point she panicked and let go the rope and just dropped fifteen feet the ground with a solid thud.

She lay on the ground moaning. "Oh dear, oh dear!" What had we persuaded Blanche to do. "We should never have done it."

I was appalled, partly because I was responsible and partly because I could not think how she could have been daft enough to let go. Luckily for everyone she only sprained her ankle.

When Aunt Nancy came back from wherever she had been she was just relieved she was not having to write to England explaining how Blanche had broken her neck. Needless to say I got a severe telling off. Here it was again. "Lou, what does thy conscience tell thee about behaving in this way?"

Later, when I returned to England, I was to learn about my father's experiences in the Fire Service. Perhaps joining the Fire Service was a bad choice of activity for his non-combatant duties because he did not like heights so was no good at going up the ladders. He maintained the solution on the part of the Fire Service was to make him an officer.

He always enjoyed telling stories against himself. At one time his job was to drive a van to a fire with a pump hitched to the back. The siren went and he dashed down to the Plymstock Fire Station checked the pump was there and drove to a fire, this time only to find a hay rick ablaze. He went to the back of the van, no pump. Someone had not put the pin in!

One of the worst experiences for him and many firemen on the east side of Plymouth was when some oil tanks at Turnchapel were set alight by incendiary bombs. They fought the fire for a long time and lost some men. The contents of one of the tanks was so low they could not reach with their equipment to put the fire out. The men knew that when the tanks were as low as this the gas collected at the base and there was an increased the risk of explosion. Nevertheless, two men climbed down into the tank and managed to extinguish the fire at unbelievable risk of their lives. They were awarded the George Medal for their gallantry.

CHAPTER TWENTY-EIGHT

Horses

RIDING HORSES AND BEING around horses and ponies was always part of my life both in England and in America. At home in Elburton before I was evacuated I would occasionally get rides on Tommy, the horse my mother rode. Tommy was a very good natured bay horse kept mostly in the field behind the house. There were stables at the Vineries and behind my grandfather's house

Louise and John riding Tommy, Mother is leading

Louise and John

next door to Tobo but because the weather in the West Country is so mild only infrequently were the horses kept inside. Besides being available for Mother to ride Tommy was used to pull cultivators such as a harrow inside the glasshouses and sometimes in light cultivations on the fields surrounding the glasshouses, or pulling the hay wain in summer. The heavy work such as ploughing was done by carthorses.

It was a special treat to be allowed to have a ride on Tommy. I would be lifted up to what seemed very great height, have my feet tucked into the leathers holding the stirrups because my short legs could not possibly reach the stirrups themselves, and hold on to the saddle while Mother or Father would hold the leading rein. In the way that animals seem to have a fifth sense about their riders, there was a story in the family of when I was riding Tommy without the leading rein and I slipped off. As soon as I hit the ground he stood stock still until I was rescued from the dangerous position underneath him close to his hooves with their metal shoes.

To get opportunities to ride horses in America was equally treasured. Daniel Collins a member of Richard and my class at school had four horses and, if we were lucky, we would get a chance to ride the smallest one called Cocoa. One of the joys at summer camp was the chance to have riding lessons, a gift from Grandmother Wood.

Besides this, Patsy Perkins from next door owned a pony, Topsy. Topsy was used to pull a little trap, so after school we would hitch her up and go for a ride, usually with pet dogs on board to join the fun. It was in this we joined the Memorial Day Parade boasting a mode of transport not needing gas.

Topsy was an old long suffering much loved pony who we all enjoyed being with, especially when having pony trap rides. Richard who was of a more thoughtful nature would like to quietly groom Topsy when he wished to avoid the rest of the noisy female household. It was a sad day in the Fall of 1942 when she succumbed to a short illness and died. For Patsy it was a terrible blow coming just after another even worse calamity when only two weeks earlier her father had died very suddenly and unexpectedly.

Aunt Nancy describes the incident graphically.

Russell Perkins, our next door neighbour and Father of the omnipresent Patsy, seemed in the best of health and spirits and told us that he was expecting to play tennis with Dick's Uncle in the afternoon. Later, at about 4:00pm the son, Eddie, dashed in and asked Dick to drive him to the club as word had come that his Father was ill and perhaps dead. Dick, of course, took him at once. I dashed in to take charge of their house as Helen, the Mother, and the two grown up daughters were away paying a call. It was a terrible thing, so sudden.

Russell had called to ask the score and Alec, Dick's Uncle, had answered with a facetious remark and turned to look at him and, in that second, he had crumpled onto the court, had a terrific haemorrhage and died even before Emlyn Stokes, their doctor opponent, could reach him across the court. Luckily the newly married daughter was at home and a fine comfort and support to her Mother.

Later in the letter Aunt Nancy comments on her relief that the Perkins were not likely to move as a result of this misfortune because she finds them 'comfortable neighbours' and Patsy a 'nice congenial' child. Patsy as the youngest in her family by several years often lived more at our house than her own, added to which she was not infrequently held responsible for leading Blanche astray on such contentious issues as bedtimes and going to the movies.

As I grew older I gained another friend who had a horse and she and I did a lot of riding together. Because we were both fairly slight, we would ride "double", either both bareback or the one in front in the saddle and the one behind without. Esther lived further out in the country near Grandmother Wood and Uncle Charlie, so there was plenty of countryside to ride around.

I report one of these trips:

Last weekend I spent Saturday night with Ester. Es has a horse which we groomed and rode. Before supper on Friday we rode in the woods, double. We came to a stream , the horse balked so I got off, she balked again so Es got off and had to lead her across. She made a beautiful jump. When I went across I got my foot wet.

On Saturday Es rode me over to Aunt Anna's and Uncle Charlie's for Saturday night. On the way over we went through an apple orchard where nearly all the apples were off the trees except for a few which we intended to get. In our efforts my overnight clothes bag fell off so I got off to get it. I picked it up and gave it to Es, then I got on again. Then, Babe the horse, went under some very low branches. I bumped my head on one and another knocked me off. It was very funny.

The real problem was always trying to get back on the horse especially if we were bare back when there wasn't anything to hang on to as well as having to persuade the horse to stand still while we struggled to get up on her back.

There were other horse adventures with Esther. I remember visiting her in the summer when we decided to sleep out in the horse's field under the stars in just our sleeping bags. Fear of rain was not a problem. We just lay stretched out on the hard ground away from the house with only a view of the stars twinkling in the dark sky as we went to sleep. We were woken in the early hours of the morning to hear horses hooves thumping on the ground around us as Babe galloped around the field as a free spirit. We just huddled together and hoped the horse would see us and not trample us under foot in the half light before the sun came up.

Earlier, in the winter, we had hitched the horse to two sleds and enjoyed being pulled all round the countryside.

Then there was the time when I purloined Richard's bike and rode from Moorestown across to Esther's home five miles away to spend the day riding Esther's horse. It rained all day and I had to be fetched home by car using valuable gas in the process. This was in the Spring of 1944 and about the same time I wrote home as follows:

Where is Tommy these days, I have not heard you speak of him? I have been going riding for the last few days (double) with a friend, Esther Wilson, who owns and cares for a horse. She is only a year older than me but my size and grade. Remember this item for I love horses. I have a plan that I am going to work on the farm and vineries when I get home and earn (me) some money to buy a horse with. Esther's horse is Tommy's colouring, I think. Tommy has a black mane and tail doesn't he?

Luckily this item was not forgotten as I shall tell.

CHAPTER TWENTY-NINE

Uncle Charlie

U NCLE CHARLIE was my favourite person in the extended
Wood family. He encouraged my love of nature and the countryside. He was a professional engineer, President of a company whose factory made the machine tools used for the manufacture of
cardboard boxes, but his hobby was archaeology and colonial history.
His wife Aunt Anna was Grandfather Wood's sister and they lived in a
charming house next door to Grandfather and Grandmother Wood in
the country about 5 miles from Moorestown in a village called Cin-
naminson which mother described when she saw it as "a perfect house
that is refinement itself." It was also a very welcoming household
where I was assured of a good time when I went to visit. The added
advantage of staying there was having the attention of two concerned
adults which I much appreciated after the hurly burly of the large
family in Moorestown.

Uncle Charlie had an interest and understanding of the natural sciences and in this role could answer my endless stream of questions. My
mother when she arrived described him as a delightful talented con-
noisseur. My greatest joy was to spend time with him at the back of his
house where he had a wooden cabin that housed his many Indian and
other archaeological artefacts many of which today are housed in the
Trenton Museum. (Trenton is the State capital of New Jersey.) Besides
these, the cabin housed a collection of furniture and household items
from Colonial times, some of which have likewise found a home in a
local historic house illustrating the early years of American life now

Uncle Charlie and Aunt Anne's house next door to Grandmother

open to the public. It was he who was able to tell me what the round grey furry ball I found under a tree one day was. It was an owl pellet disgorged after the owl had had a nice meal of mouse. Inside the ball contained all the indigestible parts he did not like and spat out. I took great delight in pulling it apart to find all the little mouse bones wrapped up in the grey fur.

Besides the Indian arrowheads, there were other Indian trophies such as an Indian tomahawk and real Indian moccasins decorated with beads, all with a tale to tell. Could the tomahawk really have been used to collect a white man's scalp? What a shuddery thought. Then there were the snowshoes, rather flat spoon shaped objects made from a bent wood frame criss-crossed with leather straps which would stop you from sinking into soft snow. I was even allowed to try them on one occasion, not so easy as it was like trying to walk with fat skis and very easy to trip up.

Uncle Charlie was in his seventies, when I knew him not a particularly tall man but with a goatee beard and laugh lines around his eyes indicating his genial nature. I have come across a letter he wrote to his mother dated 11th September 1887 when he was at Westtown Boarding School (where my sister was to go). It describes in beautiful copperplate hand an expedition he took with a group from school on horseback to look for minerals taking in on the way the famous battle field at Valley Forge. He talks in glowing terms of his finds of galena, zinc blende, brown spar, quartz and pyromorphite. He became my mentor. It is no surprise to have developed interests of a similar nature when I had such a knowledgeable and educated mind to guide me. Hence my lifelong interest in geology.

Uncle Charlie had a sense of humour too. It is with great relish I wrote home.

> *"I'll tell you a joke Uncle Charlie tells about Edgar Bergen and Charlie McCarthy, his mechanical doll.*
> *Edgar Bergen: 'Now I want an explanation and I want the truth.'*
> *Charlie: 'You can't have both.'*
> Another interesting quote is: *Every time a piece of machinery comes in the window some of our wits go out the door."*

From Uncle Charlie I heard the stories of how the early Pioneers settled America and trekked westward in the search for new farmlands. The tales of the covered wagons full of family and possessions pulled by oxen right across the deserts and mountains to California enduring hardship of hunger and hostile Indians all along the way, captured my imagination and Uncle Charlie would describe their exploits to me. The stories I read then were about the "Oregon Trail" or the "Sante Fe Trail", stories of the pioneers taking either the Northern or Southern route over the Rocky Mountains, each way with its own particular hazards. The wagons often had a painting on the canvas side telling their destination, such as "California or Bust".

One of the last things I did before leaving America was to build a wooden model Covered Wagon with "Tobo or Bust" painted on the side and this I gave to Uncle Charlie. It gives some indication of my frame of mind with the prospect of my return to England becoming ever closer. It was this inevitable return I had lived with all my time in America but I wonder if I was aware just how much of an upset it was going to be.

CHAPTER THIRTY

Planning our return

A S AN EVACUEE I knew that sooner or later I would go home to England. Day to day this was not a problem as I was extremely happy where I was in Moorestown and was not in a hurry to return. I had only rarely felt much in the way of homesickness and it hadn't lasted long. The longer my stay went on the more distant became my memories of life in England. This was a matter of much greater importance for my two sets of parents so naturally it was a subject for discussion in their letters crossing the continuingly dangerous waters of the Atlantic Ocean.

As early as November 1942 when there was still no end to the War in sight and its progress was not going well for the Allies, Aunt Nancy was writing:

> *I think of you and the children a great deal. They seem very happy, well acclimatised to their school groups and school work but I think, all the same, whether they should go home next summer. Actually I don' t think of it for our sake or their sake, but for the sake of your family membership and unity. I think if they were to come home now, or rather next summer, they would slip back into place so that they would soon seem never to have been away, except for B's physical sturdiness and a certain horrible American twang which would soon wear off if they were not with children using it. The children, of course, have no idea that I even think of this and are making great plans for extending our livestock next year but I think it would be as well for us to begin to have it in our minds at least.*

She continues later in the same letter.

Of course, I should most of all prefer to have you come to fetch them and stay a while to grow into their background here so their Americanisms would not jolt you too much. Whatever happens let's just keep our minds alert to the opportunities. Of course, their going home would be our great loss, for they feel like our children now and we would miss them fearfully. They do not love us as they do their own family and I think all the growing possible should be done in the security of that family love. It gives them a spiritual something that no amount of affectionate regard such as they have from us can supply. (We did in fact love her dearly. She may have written in this way to avoid upsetting our parents.)

Naturally you know your own situation better than we can and whether food, heat and air raid conditions will be adequate by then, not to mention the question of transportation and, of course, we cannot tell whether the situation of the world will have increased in tension by then, or have struggled through the crisis. Whatever comes let us think of it as a faint chance and have our own minds alert to consider ways and means should such a possibility arise.

The response from England to these suggestions were positive.

I am so thankful to have your letter written after receiving my effusion about the children's eventual return. I had worried for fear you might have been upset by it after I had mailed it. I am so profoundly thankful now that I sent it and that we see alike on the subject. I am continually thankful that we are so usually in fundamental agreement.

By the summer of 1943 victory over the Germans in North Africa had been achieved and a gradual reduction of the impact of the U boats in the Atlantic was taking effect. Then Benito Mussolini, the Italian leader, fell. In the beginning of August 1943 a letter arrives for my mother from Aunt Nancy commenting on this:

The world seems to be falling apart around us. I had no notion Benito's fall would have such a profound reverberations. I have told B to begin to realise that she has only one more year in our school in all probability.

Don't forget you are coming to us as soon as travelling is allowed, for a long visit and a rest and a chance to size us all up so that you can help the young readjust. I was talking to a girl from abroad last week and she said she thought readjustment would be far quicker and easier under 15 years. I think you better come about May 1st so as to see our school in action.

Whoever she was she was quite right, but it was not just age that made the difference but the length of time away as I shall show. Besides, our bond by then was more than just "affectionate regard" but great love, whatever Aunt Nancy might say to assuage my mother's feelings.

Signs of the effort my mother was now putting in to trying to arrange her visit to America is shown by a hand written letter she received from an "Intergovernmental Committee" underlining the problems she was up against.

INTERGOVERNMENTAL COMMITTEE

Sir Herbert Emerson G.C.I.E. K.C.S.I. C.B.E.
Director
11d Regent
London
7 X 43

My Dear Joan Lawson,
The person in charge of matters concerning British children abroad is Miss Maxse or her assistant, Miss Nunn, in the Children's Overseas Reception Board, Dominions Office, Devonshire. They have a representation in the British consulate at New York.

My informant in the Foreign Office emphasizes, what you and I know already, that transportation is likely to be very scarce and costly. Let me know if you think I can help further. It was good to see you both the other day.

Patricia Murphy Malin

On the back of this letter in pencil is a list of what looks like people who need to be contacted in working the way through the red tape.

Shipping Company
Passport Office
Rep. of Ministry of War Transport
United States Committee
Document to be signed with our consent for their return via North Atlantic Route
Cooks price for Portuguese Route £250

Another avenue that may have been explored was to become part of an official Quaker group sent from Meeting for Sufferings in London to the American Yearly Meeting.

In a letter of November 1943 as well as various other lines to approach there is the suggestion such as going by a merchant ship and a more resigned attitude creeps in:.

> *Now about next Spring. Don't wear yourself out worrying about details. If it is right for the children to come home and if you can come over so much the better for you and for them. If it does not work out we will go along a step at a time until we can see further. At present it looks as if the horizon might lighten by spring.*
>
> *I think you will be pleased with both girls when you get them back, but don't expect little children or treat them as such. I have grieved all along that you should miss the transition years for it is so hard to realize it has happened unless you have lived it with them. Blanche has put on more inches and has a bit of a figure and a very gracious presence when she wants to appear well and even Lou is stretching out. She is about an inch taller than B was when they first came to us and wears clothes a size bigger than B did at that time. She is getting steadily better at using her hands When she has a sick day she works on airplane models, or bead work or painting or sewing or knitting and never runs out of occupation. Her work at school is good as usual, but could be better if she were slower and more careful.*

The letter concludes:

> *Be sure if you come you give us at least 3 months, partly as a rest for you but mostly for a treat for me and so you can get the feeling of my rather*

unmethodical household and know how to make allowances for your daughters' Americanisms and get the flavour of their past 4 years of education. I shall expect you to visit classes and go to baseball games and generally be the model parent after a few weeks of idle life. School will be out about June 5th so allow all the time before that you can. Our Yearly Meeting begins the last Monday in March if you could make that it would be perfect.

Louise and Blanche March 1944

I just cannot imagine my mother at a baseball game. I wonder if she did go.

By the spring of 1944 still no progress had been made in getting a passage from England to America so it looked as if we would be in Moorestown for another whole school year. Anne was due to go to Bryn Mawr and Aunt Nancy whose health was suffering at this time (she had been diagnosed as having anaemia), decided that without Anne, her extra pair of hands, she would find looking after the "Young" as she called us three youngest children altogether too tiring. Plans were put in train for Blanche to go to boarding school; added to that was Blanche's adolescent behaviour as shown by the "movie episode".

That summer Blanche writes "On August 29th Lou and I will have been in Moorestown **FOUR** years. Do you **THINK** we will **EVER** get **HOME?**"

The discussions continue. Would mother be here for Christmas? Blanche got settled in her boarding school at Westtown and really loved it. But what about schools when we returned to England and how would our American years effect us? By October 1944 it would seem more hopeful news was coming through, but nothing definite. The Allied Invasion that had taken place in June 1944 was fighting its way eastwards bit by bit and people assumed victory was only a question of time.

In January 1945 Blanche writes:

I am glad to hear you have progressed in getting things set for coming over here. I knew you had been working on it. ...Mother you make me very amazed because you don't realize how old I am! Oh well.

Later in February she continues:

Mother we are waiting and hoping to see you very soon. Its going to be great fun having you here. Lou has no idea that you have made any progress and I guess she won't be told for fear she will get her hopes too high.

By March 1945 I knew that mother was coming and Blanche and I were getting excited at the prospect. There were also discussions now about schooling when we got home to England. Blanche comments, *If I stay in America I would finish school in June 1947 at the age of 17 years.* She half hoped this might be possible but in her heart of hearts knew her parents would want her home.

"Blanche", I asked, "Do you think we will know her when she gets here?"

"Oh I expect so." she replied. "But I'm not happy at leaving my friends, Patsy and Shona, and all the gang at school; I do love being at Westtown. What sort of English school will I end up in do you think. It could be horribly strict."

Letters written in May 1945 were written with no certain knowledge that they wouldn't pass my mother in mid-ocean coming the other way. Instructions had been sent earlier about how to deal with the American telephone system and not to let the operator confuse Moorestown with another more familiar place called Morristown. The long awaited arrival was imminent.

CHAPTER THIRTY-ONE

Mother's arrival

T HE LAST LETTER from Aunt Nancy to my mother was written on 7th May 1945 as the fighting was stopping in Europe the day before VE Day when the Allies were celebrating the end of hostilities against Germany. This was written not knowing if it would reach my mother before she left to come to America to collect us.

She writes:

I have not been writing during the last month thinking that you would not get a letter from me, but now as time passes, and you don't come I am sending along a note and hope it passes you in mid-ocean.

My heart is in my mouth today as word has come in of the stopping of the fighting. Somehow the thought of quiet and the thought of those poor souls being able to sleep and knowing no planes are coming over makes us who have never heard a hostile plane feel very humble. The services are all going to be of a religious nature - but I suppose there will be some wild celebrations in town tonight. The children get a holiday tomorrow and would like to go in town to see the celebration; but I hardly think we shall. (It would have seemed inappropriate for the family to celebrate in this way, an event that had brought so much suffering and hardship to so many people on all sides of the conflict. This was an occasion for great thankfulness more than anything else.)

On June 3rd 1945 nearly a month later there was a telephone call from Montreal. My mother had come to fetch me.

Becca took the phone call from my mother and after an initial talk passed the phone to me. The voice I heard was in this very precise English for which I had no memory at all. Was this my mother? My emotions were all mixed up. I disappeared upstairs to be on my own and have a quiet weep. I was excited and very apprehensive at the prospect of meeting my mother. I had lived all my time in America knowing where I really belonged was in England with my parents. After all, I had written and received letters all during this time which kept this fact alive in my mind. However, I was very happy where I was, I loved the Wood family as if they were my own, I had no recognition of this foreign English voice from the woman who was my mother, and she was going to arrive tomorrow, oh dear. My mind was saying one thing and my heart another.

The next day, Sunday, Blanche was recalled from her boarding school and we dressed up to go and meet the stranger on the phone at Philadelphia station. We met and yes, she still was a stranger though after a minute or two there was some recognition. Did we hug and kiss I do not remember. Sadly we had never been a demonstrative family. Was this my mother? If it was she had definitely shrunk. Now, she was shorter than my sister and not a lot taller than I was.

As Blanche said, "I didn't recognise her, Lou. Did you? But it's all coming back to me fast." The same severe hairstyle, dark hair parted in the middle and pulled back in a bun at the back of her head, the same blue eyes and neat way of dressing.

We talked a "blue streak" (non-stop) as Blanche described it, trying to fill this great gap between us. Gradually over the next weeks, more recognition would develop but it was going to be slow. How were we ever going to become a mother and daughter again? My feelings for Aunt Nancy were that of a daughter to a mother and now I was face to face with my real mother. Where was the relationship one to the other now?

After this last letter from Aunt Nancy there were still bundles of letters written to England but these are from my mother to my father reporting on what she finds once she arrives in America. Her first impressions, reactions and experiences while in Moorestown meeting the Wood family and arranging our return are all contained in these letters. There are also one or two which I and Blanche wrote to our father at this time but now the bundles include letters from my father to his wife while she was away.

Mother's letter of our first encounter mirrors my great feelings of angst at our situation. She writes on the day of her arrival:

> 272 West Main Street
> Moorestown 0169J

Dearest,

We have met and it will be quite impossible for me to describe our two beloveds. We berthed at Montreal at 12:30 on Saturday and by 3 o'clock we reached the station and straight away I got your cable off. The next job was the phone call through to Moorestown which took a long time. Becca was there to answer it and she called Louise to the phone.

It was really impossible to get any scrap of likeness into her voice that I could recognise, just incredibly impossible. Blanche's voice is perhaps not so marked by American and unrecognisable. (She would later change her mind on this when she tried talking to Blanche on the phone at school and found she could not understand her at all. She continues) *Meeting them today they were instantly spotted instantly: B. is bottled down and scared, watching me like a cat a mouse, Lou's eyes are full of affection and Blanche is lovely. We shall get on well when she can learn to open up to me and some of her excessive accent rolls off.*

This first note was followed by one written late that night.

The little scribble was really to help Blanche to write you a wee note with the enlargement of her photo which had then come in. There was much talking and piano and gramophone and 3 dogs, who seem to be Louise's special care, she did not get much down to say to you. Indeed I am a complete stranger to them, someone who has to be sized up and learnt and understood in just the same sort of way. For Blanche, poor darling, that is going to be a much harder task than for Louise who seems to accept me without question. Blanche is distinctly nervous of me but some of it rolled away towards the end of the afternoon when she had to return to Westtown.

Nancy and the two were at the station to meet me both so nicely dressed and not in this incredible noisy flummery style which is prevalent here. I got in at 10.45 and when we reached here after a 10 mile car ride I was talked to by a rather frighteningly clever group of Becca's undergraduate friends, three of them. I could hardly understand a word they said. The conversation game is to ascertain your opponents exact knowledge on every subject. I was very low down and floored. To me their references were unintelligible.

Anne is charming and indeed so is Becca.

We have been to visit Grandmother Wood, she is benevolence itself and wholly unfrightening, unlike those girls of this morning. Then next to Uncle Charlie and Aunt Anna, who live next door. I've met several other people beside to whom I've had to be excitedly introduced.

*Another topic of conversation has been Vigurs and Julia. (*Vigurs was my mother's oldest brother and his wife. This story I have already told but now it was re-examined all over again.*) An incredible coincidence of a nature that is filled with horror has come out. When they visited the Woods that time bringing those expensive and well thought out presents Julia arrived magnificently dressed in silver fox furs etc. Before she had gone she and Nancy Wood had recognised one another. Before her marriage she had been a servant in Aunt Nancy's parents house from where she had had to be evicted with the help of detectives for stealing quite considerable quantities of their silver and clothes and other things. Whether Vigur's knows of this mutual recognition or not, or of Julia's past histories who can tell. But the horror of it is a burning humiliation.*

The fact that there was a portrait of Aunt Nancy's father hanging over the fireplace in the living-room would have made it difficult for Julia to have been unaware of the household she was in. She had been a young Irish immigrant at the time. Certainly nothing was said to my mother by either party acknowledging their connection until now. My mother then goes on to say: *"I can only hope that Vigurs does not know or else that his life has been one of trying to reclaim her. Sure she has been a millstone both to herself and to him."*

The letter goes on to describe us to my father:

Louise is much the same. She has a brain. She is quick and totally lacking in patience. The things she makes, is hatching in her mind to make and the clutter that goes with all that is legion. She is far better at it than I should think I ever was at that age. She equals Barbara Wills for her inventiveness. (Barbara was a cousin of mine.)

When I asked her what she wanted to do she said she wanted to be a Window Dresser. When I unguardedly expressed surprise I think she was hurt and distressed. They think she is clever on the scholastic side and that she could easily get A's in all her school subjects if she would knuckle down to it all. Quite clear it is that she is a most exciting character and with your embracing passionate and lovable nature. Her face though longer than it was is just the same, just as swarthy and her hair is the same colour.

The girls look bloomingly well. The suggestion that Blanche is really wanting to help you with the Vineries is, I think, something to be very happy about. She is quite as tall as Joan Fox, (a contemporary of Blanche's back in England) *firmly and beautifully built not too heavy in the legs, only thoroughly solid. She had on a jolly flowered cotton frock picked out in navy blue with a light weight coat and black suede court shoes. Her hair is rather longish and she turns it inward at the bottom; it is generally rather untidy but it suits her age and height and when she learns to brush it more it will look well. Nancy seems to want her to have it permed but as it is seems alright to me.*

How I long that you could be sharing these dear children and people with me.

>*Thine always,*
>*Joan*

In the next letter written five days later we get a closer look at Nancy Wood, the woman who has cared for her children all this time:

The rush this week has made it impossible to get time to myself in which to write. Nancy has given herself over to me, it has been a non-stop run of introducing me to all her friends, taking me to functions, public and private and with it all her capacity for conversation has been equal to two or three Katkovs. (A very talkative friend of my mother's). *I'm finding the never ending stream of conversation not so trying or tiring now as I did but the first few days were hard on that count. She has either a great energy or else is using her nerves to their fullest. I would think it is the latter.*

The time for turning in at night for her is never earlier than 12:30 with the consequence that most of the morning hours are wasted. The atmosphere and place is very similar to Tigh na Crich. (The carefree house of some cousins). *The furniture of the living rooms not much better than there and the bedrooms about the same as there. But Nancy and I are getting on well - I think. I am trying to take a quiet a place behind her with regard to the children.*

Their Americanism is so complete that it would be both foolish and unkind to restrain and alter it. Much the best, and I should think the only way, is for it to drop off naturally in England and for them to mould themselves to the English pattern by the sheer force of example of English behaviour which they will see around them there. Their mannerisms and modes of dress, more than almost the methods of living and thinking are other planetary.

I was surprised when I first read this letter after my mother's death encouraged that she had realised that there was a need for this way forward, a way forward that had been rationally worked out. Certainly while we were still in Moorestown and she still a stranger to us this was the approach she took; of standing back and not coming between us and Aunt Nancy. Once back in England her less rational nature took over and she found it extremely hard to wait for our Americanisms to just "drop off naturally". As time went on she became more and more resentful of our 'Americanisms'.

She continues: *It is well nigh impossible to get time to write to you, to phone Blanche or to companion Louise. Nancy or household duties or the necessity to study the art of keeping cool takes up every minute. Nancy is a bit wearying, though I like her ever-so much and we get on well together. She talks unendingly, contradicts and argues much more than I and her ideas and methods of organising are always best. I don't wonder there have been difficulties for Blanche. But in essence it is wonderful how similar are our standards of behaviour, of religion and world politics.*

The next weeks in America were going to be a great strain for my mother and Aunt Nancy. They were both in a most uncomfortable situation with regard to each other. Did it help that mother was able to see our American home? How would she have felt about it if she had not visited us in Moorestown? Was the endless talk from Aunt Nancy a response to this stressful relationship?

CHAPTER THIRTY-TWO

Mother's journey

ONCE MOTHER HAD arrived we heard about her journey from England which had been quite as eventful as ours five years before. Her journey took fifteen days nearly twice as long as we had taken. She left Cardiff on Thursday 17th May 1945 in the evening on a small cargo boat, The *Lochmonar*, which took a few passengers. Victory in Europe had been celebrated nine days before she left so it is a little surprising to find that her voyage was to be taken in convoy with a group of other ships of all shapes and sizes, from ships even smaller than themselves up to an aircraft carrier.

She writes a long letter, added to regularly as the long journey elapsed, filling the vacant days on board ship knowing it could not be posted until she reached the other side of the Atlantic:

23rd May 1945

Dearest,

The first day was calm and foggy and by Friday some one dropped a depth charge and all the boats changed their course in one direction and another like a lot of kittens turning round. Then there were two boat drills we had to go through. By Saturday we had got into windy weather and I disappeared below to stay until Wednesday. We are beginning to roll again, carrying only ballast does not help but there is no doubt that the Lochmonar is a well found boat and there is little vibration. The food too is good and the bedroom steward friendly. I've had all his story and now on hearing of Churchill's resignation we talk rebellious politics.

What I have seen of our companion ships is a most amazing sight. One day when I had forced myself on deck for a while a very rusty coal driven boat that had been rather panting alongside us all the way developed engine trouble. It seemed to stand stock still then listed and came right across close behind our stern. By then she was broadside on to the swell and there we had to leave her. That left consternation among us unhardened passengers as no relief ship turned up to her rescue and finally after half a day she righted her trouble and slowly caught up alongside again. The Captain looks on her as a menace. We have many days ahead of us and do not expect to arrive as soon as they optimistically told us in Cardiff.

My continual thought has been with what B and L had to go through when they went out and I am glad for their sakes that I am having something of a taste of it. We don't expect to get in under the fortnight, particularly as we get slowed down by banks of fog but that keeps the sea very calm so we put up willingly with the distraction of the devastating foghorn.

Our company of ships is as varied as our fellow passengers but many times greater. Indeed it would be a tedious journey were it not that we could survey both. We all have our minds turned on our arrival and are beginning to wish it nearer. Very little daily news bulletins get through to us so we know neither the condition of the sea or the land. We just go relentlessly on and on at times totally alone in a world of fog and then it clears or we sail through it to find a warm sea covered by our boats.

I've been talking several times with the Canadian widow and her attractive son Jeremy. They are going right to Victoria but she will have the helpful company of Canon Rowe, a benevolent and broadminded Churchman. Mrs Martin (my cabin mate) is most anxious that he should convert me to a more definite belief in the 'after life' and to that end the three of us had a long discussion in the lounge last evening while several of the rest of the company made much use of the bar.

Rumours and romances abound. There are no less than six American brides or brides to be ranging from one 50 year old woman to a pretty Welsh girl. The incompetent mother of the youngest baby is married to a lawyer and is going to live in Texas where she will be a neighbour of Mr.Bible, also a passenger, (was that really his name or one she made up for him?) who says he will be no nearer to her than a hundred miles - smile not. He says she little realises what she has to face, for when she arrives she will be greeted by sandstorms and mosquitoes. One's only thought is for that poor baby, how can *it hope to survive?*

There is a Texan who is most interesting once you can prize open his lips. He has been to England in the capacity of a water engineer, or rather Scotland, where I think he was disgusted at the conservative landlords who tried to bloc against the creation of dams and the extension of tracts of new water. It is a vexed question. Some of the locals were audacious enough to argue that the Moors must be preserved for the shooting, the rivers for the fish and that seemed more important to them than the preservation of the beauty. But from what we have read of the T.V.A. (Tennessee Valley Authority, which was established by Roosevelt as part of his "New Deal" during the American Depression in the early 1930,s which involved building many dams to improve the quality of life in that part of the United States.) *I'm inclined to think that the beauty would not be lost but would take another aspect and water would be led to all the thousand villages that are so terribly needing it.*

How I wish and the girls will wish, that you were to share in our meeting. It can hardly be measured. My cup would have been really brimming if you could be with us. Dearest I yearn for you, my heart has been so full of love for you."

> Thine,
>> *Joan*

Though my mother had been away from home on her own before, this will have been the first time in her life when she will have been away from my father on her own for so long and so far away.

Soon the message was coming through that Montreal would be the point of disembarkation and not Halifax as was originally suggested. The letter is quite a long one but sadly pages are missing and these are the ones that relate the dramatic incident in the convoy as it crossed the Grand Banks into the St. Lawrence river. Much was said, and this together with the memory of the tale we heard when mother reached New Jersey, enables me to put the story together.

The Grand Banks, off the east coast of this part of America are notorious for fog and icebergs and the convoy met both, as we had on our voyage. Orders were given to change course and then to change course again. Unfortunately not all ships received both messages and chaos ensued as all the ships began moving in differing directions. The outcome was that two ships went on an iceberg, the Commodore's own Corvette and one of the freighters. Twelve ships were in collision. The convoy became dispersed over an area of 18 miles and the morning after the night of the incident the passengers of the Lochmonar woke up to see not a single ship on the sea around them. It took all day for the convoy to get back in formation, The *Lochmanar* actually sailing back towards England to achieve this. The small freighter that had been their constant companion for so long stayed away to stern and never caught up again. No casualties were reported but rumour had it that an aircraft carrier passed within inches of their little ship. How lucky she was.

While my mother was crossing the Atlantic my father now started writing regularly to her in Moorestown. To begin with he was still awaiting news of her arrival there. Now that he had at last put pen to paper he comments in one of his letters that perhaps he too should have written to us during the time we were away. How Blanche yearned to have a letter from him during our time in Moorestown, certainly she in particular had begged him on more than one occasion to do so. One of the first goes as follows.:

Tobo
Elburton
Devon
23rd. May 1945

Dearest Joan,
I keep wondering how you are getting on, if you are sick or having a good crossing.

By the time you get this you will have met Blanche and Louise. I shall love getting a letter from you telling me if they are just the same. I don't know why but I am most interested to know how the Americans react to you. I feel just a little lost without you. This should please you quite a bit.

I am still feeling a little tired after all the excitement of getting you off. I feel just a bit like I used to as a child when I would be in a big field all by myself. Just rather fun being on your own but a feeling of no one to fall back on. All the same people are very good to me.

Love dearest Joan.
Tell Blanche I shall never forget the kiss she gave me when she left England.

Just a big hug. Do Louise's eyes look just the same?
    Love to all,
        Francis

This and many of the letters my mother received during the time she was visiting America give news from the Channel Islands which had now been liberated. A number of my father's closest relatives had lived in Guernsey throughout the Occupation and stories were now arriving telling how they had fared during this time. The Islanders had been relieved that the Germans had not decided to fight the liberating army because Guernsey was a veritable fortress which if called to action would have had a devastating effect. Life in Guernsey during the Occupation has already been documented so it is not my task here to retell these stories.

My father's particular concern was what he could do to get their glasshouse businesses up and running once more by seeking assistance for them from Ministries in London.

CHAPTER THIRTY-THREE

Last days of American school

M OTHER ARRIVED JUST a week before school ended for the summer that year when I was thirteen. She was just in time to visit the school and attend some of the end of year events. The first event she attended was the last morning assembly of term when the school received their class and games prizes. Afterwards I came up to the adults of the family who were attending.

"Look, Mummy, I've been given a second team badge because I won't be here next year to get one. Aren't I lucky? Will you look after it for me while I see my friends.

I don't want to say good bye to them at all. I hope I shall see some of them around town before I go. I will won't I?"

Mother reports on this event:

"Chester Reagan, the Headmaster, is spoken of highly, I thought the music master, Lou's class mistress and some of the others very good. M.F.S. seems able to keep their staff for a long time and they have a good balance of tried teachers against younger ones. L's class mistress I was really impressed with and also with the group of children in her class. From the point of view of size she is head and shoulders smaller than they. She has made good grades in her exams though she could do better if her application was more concerted (the usual story). *Mathematics seems to be something she is good at and her Latin would be good but she has no great love for the Latin master who seemed just the sort of master you would likely find in a good English Quaker School* (bad omens).

We had four women staff to supper one night. The elderly but capable,
friendly and unfrightening Miss Swan, Gwendolyn Coney, form mistress,
Mrs. Mcone, games mistress and one other older Housemistress. It helped a
lot to hear about the children from them, they are genuinely going to miss
them"

The Chairman of Moorestown Friends School as well as Chairman of
Representative Meeting (the equivalent of the English Meeting for Sufferings, the Executive of the Society of Friends in England) was Albert
Linton and as such was much respected in the town. It was the Lintons
we had expected to go to when we left five long years ago to come to
America but who at the last minute decided my sister and I were too
young for their household. Naturally my mother was very curious to
meet them. She and Aunt Nancy (Uncle Dick was away at the time)
were asked to the Lintons for dinner. She tells of this occasion.

It was, she writes:

The usual evening meal at which one is expected to eat large helpings of
*meat, ice cream and rich cakes. (*Mother, after years of rationing will
have found this quite daunting.*) The Lintons like us planted all their*
own trees and built their house with a slate roof, almost grey green like the
Delabole slate of Tobo and a good coloured brick in 1928. Decidedly
well-to-do, he is Chairman of an enormous Insurance Company. Albert
Linton, an immaculate entertaining rather mischievous man whose hobbies
are assisted by immense and perfect equipment.

Altogether quite a swell. His wife Margie is delightful and not so par-
ticular. She showed us four bird films, St Lawrence river area, California,
Florida and one other which were much superior in scope to anything we
have seen from our local experts at home. I think it is a mercy B. and L.
were not there, though the Lintons, Fran and Agnes Stokes and the Browns
at Westtown are among the nicest with whom I've so far come into close
contact.

All previous comments on our placement had endorsed the fact that we
were far better off in the Wood family so it was good for Mother to
make this confirmation for herself.

Blanche's school also finished about the same time but Mother was unable to attend any functions as they had all been cancelled due to a case of polio in the school. A member of the Senior Class had gone down with the dreaded disease and an immediate quarantine had been imposed. Infantile Paralysis, as it is also known, was a real threat in those days before the availability of vaccines to give protection. Particularly likely to appear in hot weather it could quickly spread through the children of a community leaving the victims paralysed and crippled for life or even leading to death. It was due to the fear of Infantile Paralysis that we were never allowed to visit a public swimming pool or even go to the movies during the summer time if it was thought we might be at risk.

Once the quarantine was over my mother went with Aunt Dottie Wood, an aunt of Richard and Anne's, to collect Peggy Wood, her daughter and their cousin, who was in Blanche's class at Westtown School. Parents were not allowed in the buildings and no contact with other children was permitted. Blanche and Peggy were taken right out to the ever available and reliable Grandmother Wood where they were to stay for eight days until their quarantine was over.

My mother tries hard not to alarm my father in England when she tells of this calamity even though very worried herself.

Apparently it is not usual for it to strike more than once in the same place. What does worry me a little is the lack of discipline which leaks over into everything. Very little is known about the disease or its cure. Quarantine regulations vary enormously from state to state and I was thankful that the doctor here does not take chances. But, even so, nobody thinks it important to guard the children's belongings and B's bedding and some of her laundry have been dumped on the veranda; the air being considered sufficient safeguard. B had not been with the child who has the malady very badly for more than a week before she was taken ill. Her dormitory was on another floor and she was not using the same bathrooms. So really I am not letting myself worry and I do not want you to do so either. For the school it has been a very hard blow and more than tragic for the child's parents.

Later on Mother was able to meet some of the staff of Westtown when she stayed with the Browns there.

CHAPTER THIRTY-FOUR

Blanche's year at Westtown

D URING OUR LAST YEAR in America Blanche had been away at boarding school. For her this year was the best of all her school days and she remembers it with great joy. Recently I asked her to write about it for me and this is what she sent me:

There is no doubt that I was sent to Westtown because of my adolescent behaviour. Becca and Anne were more interested in scholastic achievement, whereas I was much happier playing hockey or basketball or going ice skating in winter and playing tennis and swimming in summer. School work was definitely not one of my high priorities, I considered boys and sport much more fun.

This caused Aunt Nancy considerable concern especially the night Dave took me to the flicks, when instead of going to the Moorestown cinema he said,

"Come on, lets go to Philadelphia and see 'Happy Go Lucky'", so we hopped on a bus and off we went. All good fun, but I was a bit apprehensive as I realised no one knew where I was and we didn't get back until 11.30p.m. and I got into a lot of trouble. I think that was the last straw as far as Aunt Nancy was concerned and boarding school it should be.

Plus the fact that next door lived my great friend Patsy. Patsy about two years earlier had lost her father who died of a heart attack suddenly while playing tennis. So Patsy lived with her mother and she and I plus another friend called Shona went everywhere together. Shona was another English girl from Weston-super-Mare, whose father was in the R.A.F. and for some reason was working in America with the American Air force on bombers.

Aunt Nancy felt that Patsy's influence was not doing me much good, she was into boys in a big way and did far less work than I did, she was also good at sport. However, the two of us had a great deal of fun. It was therefore decided to send me to Westtown and it was paid for mainly by the Society of Friends. It turned out to be one the most influential years of my five in America as far as I was concerned. At Westtown I made more friendships which have lasted a life time than anywhere else.

Westtown is the wealthiest of all the Quaker Boarding Schools. Started in 1779, it today has about 600 children. It is set in West Chester County outside Philadelphia in 600 acres of campus, park and farm land. With some truly beautiful trees such as the ginko and tulip trees which made up the Granolithic Walk, which ran in front of the school. The main building was of red brick a large imposing old building with the girls living at one end and the boys living ant the other end and Central the main entrance hall in between the two ends. The class rooms were on the ground floor and the next two stories were made up of the living accommodation.

It was a well endowed school when I was there in 1944–1945 and even more so now. It now has a full size running track and full size gymnasium and swimming pool complex. The baseball pitch and the hockey pitch are still as I remember them. They also have a large new building which houses the main assembly hall and the art school. The Quaker Meeting House is the same as it was when I was there.

It was not going to be strange as there were many people from Moorestown Friends School attending as well and this made it a lot easier. We arrived in September on a fine sunny day. Aunt Nancy took me by car. The dormitories were split into rooms and there were two girls to a room. My room mate was Patsy Hussey a very good looking girl. We never became close friends, but we got along well enough.

We met again in 1997 at the 50th reunion of our class, I didn't recognise her at first, but she told me a lovely story. We used to decorate our own rooms. She and I met Aunt Nancy in Philadelphia and we bought counterpanes and a rug for the floor and acquired an easy chair, there was a bed and a desk for each of us. We used to stick up pictures of movie stars cut from magazines on the walls. Evidently I got tired of these and one day I took them all down and put them on her desk and never said a word. Patsy said she remembered the episode well I can

Blanche in 1945

only think it was very unkind of me.

My school subjects were English, history, French, (I ended up having seven French teachers in two years not much hope there, but that is another story) Latin and Algebra. Latin was a struggle and after many letters it was decided I should drop Latin. However some of it must have gone in because later in life learning the Latin names of plants was not a problem.

Algebra was not much good, I didn't like the teacher and I didn't bother to try. I never forgave him for taking away a K.O.B. A K.O.B. means "Kare of Bearer" and we used to write them from boy to girl and vice versa to ask for dates. This time the teacher took it and threw it in the waste paper basket. Another boy retrieved it for me. I wasn't paying attention, it was all so boring. A date in winter meant that in the hour after supper we could meet in the Central Hall, while in summer we could spend the same hour after supper walking up and down the Granolithic Walk. Unless there was a dance as on a Saturday night or a play in the School Hall etc., they were used by us for forms of communication with the opposite sex. Someone would hand you one and you delivered it to the addressee. They were written on A4 paper and folded in the form of a square, just fitting in the hand.

Our day started at 7.30 a.m. with breakfast, unless you were on early duty. We had a work program and everyone did an hour per day, doing some chore around the school, such as laying the tables, washing dishes, sweeping corridors. Every three weeks the chore changed and you had another duty. Laying breakfast was not a popular duty as you had to be up by 6.30 a.m. Before every meal grace was said and we had a Bible reading as well at breakfast time. Lessons started at 9.00 a.m., but before that we all had to keep our rooms clean and tidy and if a "Coody" was found underneath the bed you got a black mark. "Coody" was a ball of fluff or dust.

Lessons finished about 3.30p.m. and then we either had hockey or lacrosse in the autumn term, basketball in the winter term, and tennis or swimming in the summer term.

When we first arrived we were not allowed to go home for a month. It was great excitement on my first visit back to Moorestown for a week end. I went by train from West Chester to Philadelphia and then by bus out to Moorestown, a distance by car of 30 miles, but to cross Philadelphia on my own at 15 years, one is unlikely to let your children do it today.

When I first went to America I was in the sixth grade at Moorestown Friends School and I stayed there through ninth grade. I entered Westtown in the tenth grade, so if I had not been brought back to England I would have only had two more years of schooling to complete. It really was questionable whether they shouldn't have left me to finish my American education, but it was not to be.

Various episodes stand out in my mind, skating on the lake in winter with Peter, who was an excellent skater. Tobogganing on the run down to the lake through the woods when it snowed. Playing hockey against Moorestown Friends School. I was on the junior varsity team, that was a real highlight as I was able to see Patsy that day.

During this time Becca and Anne were both at Bryn Mawr College and Aunt Nancy only had Lou and Richard at home. Anne had done a great deal of looking after us and Aunt Nancy felt she could not cope with three of us without Anne's help, so life was easier for her.

While at Westtown I wrote to my parents in England each week. It is obvious from these letters that by this time they were complete strangers to me and I often did not know what to say. My hand writing had deteriorated considerably over the five years, which could not have pleased my mother who was a calligrapher. The Dean of Women at this time was Rachel Letchworth a dynamic person who had the respect from all the girls. I will never forget the night she told me my mother was arriving in America to take us home to England, it was the last thing I wanted to do, to leave a school I loved and all my friends. The next five years were to prove extremely difficult for me school-wise and getting to know our parents again, especially mother, was the most difficult. I really did not enjoy myself very much until I got to University.

However the friends I made during that one year at Westtown were numerous and the friendships have lasted a lifetime. Since leaving Westtown I have been back to three reunions, the last in 1997, 50 years after the class graduated. Although I never graduated they still consider me to be part of the Class of 47.

All staff were called by their first names with either Master in front for male staff and Teacher in front for female staff. One teacher should be mentioned and that is Master Carroll, he taught Senior English and his wife Anna Brown, were very good to me during that year. After the war they visited us in Plymouth and brought me the dozen Westtown plates depicting the scenes of the school and made by Wedgwood, which were I had bought earlier as a present from Rachel Cadbury a Moorestown Friend. These gave me a lasting reminder of my time there.

CHAPTER THIRTY-FIVE

Mother visits the Jameses

WHILE MOTHER WAS in New Jersey to collect us she made a number of visits to other households, partly I imagine to relieve the stress for her and Aunt Nancy while living in the same house and sharing the ownership of my sister and me. Some of these visits were within Moorestown while others were farther afield to enable her to see a bit more of the country. These stays, which she found helpful, were overnight stays of a day or two. An early visit was to the James family at Wallingford on the other side of Philadelphia from Moorestown, with whom we had spent two long summers as well as other exchanges. Mary was tall, dark eyed with shoulder length dark hair while in contrast Caroline was fair haired and decided early that she wished to train as a nurse like her mother, which suited her caring nature.

The Jameses had a big house and grounds which when put with Aunt Dottie's father's house next door made quite a small estate. They had the advantage of having a live-in family helper, Magda, already mentioned, and a younger sister and brother, Peggy and Johnnie besides Mary and Caroline who were our friends.

My mother seems to have developed a good rapport with Aunt Dottie. She comments to Dottie:

"I always worried because I wondered that the children went to the movies rather often when Blanche and Lou stayed with you, but I can see that it was something that you will have kept in perspective and I need not have worried at all."

Mother could see that this was a good wholesome Quaker family. Dottie replied:

"Yes, I can see how you may have thought that but we discussed what they saw and kept the matter within bounds. You can tell from your stay here how we can have these very wet days and thunderstorms when going to the "flicks" seems the best idea. Talking of "flicks" would you like to see the home movies we took at the pool when the weather was sunny and warm?

Caroline, you know how to work the projector. Can you set it up so we can show those pictures of you all practicing your diving to Lou's Mommy."

Mary and Caroline were both excellent swimmers and divers and we would spend hours at the Club pool near them perfecting our technique in back dives and somersaults. Mother delighted in what she saw.

"Dottie, it really was extremely kind of you to have had my girls to stay," my mother said. "I can see what a great time they had here."

"Well, you will realize that there are many people in Moorestown who have helped in differing ways in the care of the 'English Evacuees'. You will see during your stay that Nancy Wood is a great organiser and manager of everybody and everything."

"Yes, she reminds me of my elder sister, Helen, in this respect. She, like Nancy takes all the responsibility for her family while her husband, like Dick, takes a back seat on family matters. I understand she has had health problems this last year which means she must wear herself out trying to do so much. She never stops," my mother pointed out. "It's interesting that the girls soon after they arrived said that Aunt Nancy was like their Aunty Helen."

"My having Blanche and Lou here was one way of protecting Nancy from herself," Dottie replied.

This view of Aunt Nancy confirmed what my mother had found since she arrived at 272. Grandmother Wood in particular acted as her guardian angel in this respect by not only having children to stay at different times but also on the financial front as well. Aunt Nancy got on better with her mother-in-law than she did with her own mother. Similarly Uncle Charlie and Aunt Anna had frequently had me to stay over the five years and now invited Aunt Nancy away for a week's stay at Eaglesmere during this last summer while we were awaiting our passage home to England.

When visiting the Browns, at Westtown, mother was able to get a look at Blanche's school which, because of the polio quarantine, she had not been able to see at the end of the school year when she first arrived. Thus, she was able to meet the Headmaster and some of the other staff and see the magnificent country setting of this school which Blanche had enjoyed so immensely. It meant Blanche was very anxious to attend another school in the country when she got to England rather than one in a city.

Though my school was decided before my mother arrived in America, my sister's school had not. It appeared that my school had no room for her and other schools they approached which they considered suitable were giving a similar reply. The fact that Blanche was older and should be taking the School Certificate as soon as possible but had a different educational background added to the problem. Hence, my parents still had not found somewhere for her to go to by the time we left for our return to England.

My mother enjoyed her stay with the Browns even though the temperatures were now well in the 90's Fahrenheit, a humid heat at that. What she liked was the orderly household and the chance to have an afternoon rest. An afternoon rest was a long established custom for her, echoes of the life of an "Edwardian Lady". A family with only two adults was bound to be calmer than one of seven back in Moorestown. How was she going to manage her two noisy American daughters when we all got back to Tobo? Her love of calm and order was definitely going to be challenged.

It was Caroll Brown, an experienced schoolmaster, who took her aside later to say; "You realise that you must understand the great strain put on the English children by uprooting them and planting them in America. It has made them 'not normal' and hard to deal with as a result."

My mother's reply was: "Yes, I gather you have had a difficult time with one or two here at Westtown but I think perhaps you are exaggerating a little. Certainly I shall remember the shock it was for Blanche and Louise to have to face me when I arrived."

I don't think we ever fell into the category of 'not normal' but a little hard to deal with at times like most teenagers I don't doubt.

Other people she visited were Agnes Stokes, Aunt Nancy's great friend, who had helped in the organisation of the English Evacuees and who had housed one of 'our' group. Her husband Fran had a tomato factory so they found much to talk about.

Of course, she also visited my Uncle Vigurs in New York. However, one person she enjoyed particularly visiting was Rachel Cadbury, the mother of Jack who had been in touch with them when he visited England during the War. It was Jack who had recounted the 'butter' story to my parents. Rachel, I remember gave Blanche and me $10 to spend to buy a present from America to take home with us. What riches! I bought myself some oil paints and Blanche the Westtown plates.

CHAPTER THIRTY-SIX

The household

The house is old, the upstairs rooms needing to have much done to them in the way of paint and plumbing and better woodwork. The furniture is about the same level but with a leaning toward mahogany and antiques. Nothing much in the way of carpets. Whether the children's advent is the cause for this lack of attention and expenditure on the house I cannot say. The dining room is well furnished, beautiful Chippendale period chairs and table and the china is lovely. Our silver is better I should say. But children play and dogs play havoc in the lounge.

THUS MY MOTHER described 272 when she first arrived.
As time went on during her stay she became more critical of the household she found. The untidiness was something that jarred. She herself was fastidious to a point of obsession in her need for neatness and order. However, in a family of seven people and three dogs in a not overly large house this was something of a low priority.

Later in June about three weeks later she writes to my father of "Things to Disturb". These were:

the habit of meals at any and every time of day and of house cleaning and tidiness that leaves everything to be desired. These matters are not looked on as essentials or in any way fundamental and perhaps we ,or at least I, lay too much stress on them. With the adjustment of B. and L. to Tobo this is going to be one of the problems. Adding; *In Lou these things are going to be difficult to rectify but in spite of this they have given the girls real education, a sense of security and stability.*

Lucky for Blanche that she was in accord with the desire for neatness and tidiness, while my propensity to untidiness was going to be one thing that would hinder my future relationship with my mother. Though was it just my untidiness that was the problem or the fact that it was a constant reminder of my American influences that upset her so? I wonder if I would have been the same without the American experience. This sort of question would vex my mother; how different would I have been without this American experience? Meanwhile, I at that time was not of an age to worry about the world that might have been. Looking back now, I am quite sure I developed differently through this experience and benefited greatly in many ways as a result of it.

By the end of June the heavy oppressive humid high 90s Fahrenheit heat of a New Jersey summer descended on the house in Moorestown. By now I was well used to this and took it in my stride but for my poor mother it was a real trial. She was established in Becca's bedroom. Thus, Becca was up on the third floor sharing with Anne, I who at times enjoyed that room on my own was sharing with my sister in what was once called the Nursery. I enjoyed life in that room but my mother considered the bed hard, the temperatures high and though it was on the north side of the house as hot as everywhere else. In those days air conditioning was not to be found in private houses as it is today.

There was a very hot day at this time and for some reason Mother and I were alone at 272.

"Why aren't there any windows open here in the living room?" she asked. "If we had some windows open we could get a draft going through and that would make it cooler."

So she set about trying to lift the sash window to the back garden.

"I don't think you'll get it to budge." I replied. "I can't remember anyone opening that window ever."

She eventually got it open. Alas, it was not a success. The window in question faced the back of the house where the dogs had their fenced in run; the cooling breeze arrived bearing a nasty odour of dog smells. The window was hastily shut.

The letter after this on June 27, 1945 she admits;

I think in regard to lots of things I must be getting much less particular; and that should please you. I'm concerned that so much of what I have been writing you will make you worry. You know how easily and unnecessarily I do that myself. There is much to encourage ourselves with in regard to the children. Blanche is reliable in lots of ways and thoughtful for other people and she is fine about the house though she does not take to cooking. Lou does her chores in fits and starts but Blanche can carry quite a lot of responsibility.

Sadly this positive approach did not last and a few weeks later she records with horror the day one of the three dogs was horribly sick on the living room carpet. Fortunately, this uncalled for event called for drastic action and the living room carpet found its way outdoors into the back yard and onto the clothes line after appropriate cleansing and received a thorough airing. Apparently it was I who scrubbed it all over with soap and a hard brush, making a regular job of it, so it seems. Added to that, Georgie the faithful yardman was pressed into scrubbing the downstairs floors with Lysol which had the added advantage that for a short while the fleas would be kept at bay. About the same time Blanche had a vigorous anti-flea campaign on all the dogs with a similar result. The fleas in question were only sand fleas and as far as I was concerned were of no consequence, but they obviously found my mother a new and tasty target which they attacked anew after each of her visits away.

The sequel to the carpet cleaning was more horror for my meticulous mother because it was left out all week in rain and sun. Having once got wet there was bound to be problems about its return indoors, so why worry. Mother was alarmed at this casual approach.

The other problem for her was the irregular time keeping. Meals could be at any time, bedtimes were late especially for the adults, and not infrequently for the children as well. She should have expected this because many times the letters she received tell her they were being written late at night which was often the only time Aunt Nancy had peace and quiet at the end of the day in which to do it. As a consequence, breakfast could be any time up to eleven o'clock in the morning.

A family outing in July seems to have upset her.

This business of the 20th century is a problem. In what way do you think we celebrated it last night? At 9:50pm after a fairly strenuous day in one way and

another Dick offered the family a trip to the Drug Store. There we sat with all
the less disciplined of the town in a brilliantly lit saloon to partake of ices. We
waited to be served until about 10:20 and returned well filled with Sundaes of
varying richness about 11 o'clock. Sonny and Lou were there also of course.
But why couldn't we have done that at 8 or 8:30 and returned those children to
bed at a decent hour?

Needless to say Sonny and Lou were only too happy to join such a famous
outing improved in our eyes by the lateness of the hour.

In the same letter where she reports on the history of the carpet, about
six weeks into her stay in Moorestown when she was no longer being
rushed from place to place as she had at the beginning of her stay, she
describes what was a typical scene in the house.

Blanche and her two friends Shona and Patsy are making a great noise about
nothing, just roaming around. Emma is sweeping the downstairs in a desultory
fashion and she has the wireless on a non-stop show, she gives fulsome amused
chuckles at it when it pleases her. Nancy for the first time since I have been here
is dusting, tidying and cleaning upstairs while Lou after much pleading has
succeeded in being allowed to use the ironing machine. She is ironing a large
basket of 'straight linen'. Yesterday both girls worked very hard at cleaning the
back porch which is in the kind of state our woodshed is usually in. They have
made a fine job of it but this morning Emma is very sceptical because she says
it will only take a week for it to be as bad again.

Was all this cleaning activity by my sister and me just the normal run of
chores, or were we trying to impress my mother because we were aware of
her view that tidiness like cleanliness was next to Godliness, or were we
trying to help Aunt Nancy by making things better?

Even though my mother had arrived, I was spending as much time as I
could playing with my friends and not so often at 272 doing chores.
Richard was not around at this time, we hardly saw him because he was
staying on the farm of a school friend, Howdy Taylor, helping out. His
particular love was milking the cows. A love that took him into farming
later in life.

He was not the only one who did farm work. Blanche, Patsy Perkins
and myself, when I was allowed, could earn money doing piece work on
one of the local truck farms or market gardens as we would call them in

England. This would mean picking strawberries or peaches or whatever crop was in need of harvesting at the time. This meant getting up really early at 6:00a.m., being picked up by a farm truck and riding in the back out of town to the flat sandy fields where the work was. It could be strenuous work, hence I was not always allowed to do it on a regular basis. The other two did it more as they were older and stronger.

The best part about it was the money I could earn.

"Mummy, I want to buy you a dress with the money I've earned," I announced. "I know it's real difficult to buy clothes in England. Aunt Nancy says we can all have a day out shopping in Germantown where she does a lot of her clothes shopping."

So off we all went.

Mother tried on a number of different ones for us all to admire. "I like this one in the pale turquoise best. It is very discreet which I like," she said. We knew by now that she did not like many of the fancy American clothes. This dress made of the new material, rayon, had long sleeves, a turn down open collar and plain pleated skirt.

"It costs $7.95, Lou, can you really afford it?"

"Oh yes, Mummy I think it looks super."

Sadly it creased, and my ever critical mother put this as another black mark against American clothes.

CHAPTER THIRTY-SEVEN

Returning home

O NCE IN AMERICA my mother's next task was to arrange a passage home again. Towards the end of June there was a letter from a representative of the Children's Overseas Reception Board via the British Consulate in New York acknowledging the application for a priority passage home. When my mother went to visit my Uncle in New York she took the opportunity to visit the Consulate but was very worried she had upset the "'Representative" in some way partly it seems due to the fact that she should not have been in the U.S.A. at all and was not playing by the "rules" by being there.

However, she was able to assure herself that she had done all she could and that the only thing now was to sit and wait until a passage was available. This it would seem was likely to be toward the end of July. She also discovered some other English Friends, the Pickards, who were also hoping to get back to England that summer.

Thus, packing all our belongings to take home had to be organised. By the middle of July two trunks and two suitcases had already been packed. These were the same two suitcases we had arrived with, the detailed list of contents carefully pasted on to the inside of the lid. Yet another trunk would be needed as well. One advantage of travelling by boat was all those weight restrictions familiar to air travellers were not a problem, adults being allowed 448lbs., and Blanche and I 224lbs., each. Though with this amount of luggage how were we going to get to the embarkation point? Already two parcels of groceries, allowable within the regulations, had been dispatched to England containing goods either unavailable or in short supply there.

At the end of July rumours were beginning to circulate about possible boats but nothing definite was heard. The added problem was that there was no way of knowing which harbour it might leave from in the U.S.A. or even Canada, nor, at which port in Britain it would arrive. Pressure was mounting.

Blanche asked wistfully. "Couldn't I stay until I finish school? I do love it here so." Sadly for her this was never really considered as all felt she should return to her roots.

In a letter at the end of July mother dwells on the problems for us all.

> *I'm dreading the last days here, they will be at fever heat. Blanche is feeling dreadfully torn. Our biggest task is to gain their love and respect and oh, it's going to be hard. They have received me as an unpleasant necessity poor darlings and quite frankly and uncompromisingly prefer Aunt Nancy. It is hard to keep a festering jealousy from rising up inside me. Perhaps it is not jealousy but just a new sort of heartbreak that has gone with this whole business over these five years. But it is not only our own heartbreak but theirs as well. Theirs that I do not come up to their expectations, that I do not identify myself here and that modes and manners here are so obviously not ours at home.* (By now she was beginning to feel homesick and in need of my father's support and it was becoming evident that the readjustment was going to be very difficult for all concerned.)

Father, knowing this, had written around the same time,

> *It was brave of you to go to America and I feel so proud of you. I find myself talking of you often and thinking of you and the children a great deal. I had arrived at a stage when I dare not think of Blanche and Louise. I know this is the case. I remember so well how I felt in 1940. If we were going to be invaded at least we would have sent something of us into a free America.*

Thus we can see the heartbreak of my parents, facing the consequences of their decision to send their daughters away for the "Duration", little realising what would be the outcome. For my sister and me there was also heartbreak. This time the wrench from this home was much more painful. We were older, no longer small children ever trusting in the decisions of the grown ups. The sense of adventure we had on arrival was gone, only the torment of leaving a family who was very dear to us and a way of life that we thoroughly enjoyed. Neither of us was looking forward to the stricter regime of an English school.

The two things that were going to make our readjustment difficult when we did get home were my mother's jealousy of Aunt Nancy and her growing antipathy to all things American. The jealousy continued to fester, if anything it got worse as the years went by. Nor did she come to terms with the American way of life even though she had by now two American daughters who had enjoyed their American experience and benefited in so many ways from that experience.

Luckily I was unaware, two months into her stay in Moorestown, the extent of her view of America. It was only once back in England and she had us to herself once more did these feelings of antipathy develop and become more pronounced. Then she began to belittle America and all things American.

At this time an example of this approach was illustrated by an event that hit the headlines. An aeroplane had crashed into the Empire State Building. Fortunately for those inside the building, the damage to the plane was much greater than the damage to this tall skyscraper. My mother's comments when she learnt of this event which happened in August 1945: *An awful judgement on the Tower of Babel.* What prejudices of modern skyscrapers and for why?

On 8th August news came, at long last, from Cunard of passages home for us all. We were to go on the SS *Nieuw Amsterdam* of the Holland-America line leaving from Hoboken Pier, New York, on Monday 20th August 1945. This was it. **We were finally going**. The expected port of arrival was Southampton, which was good news and led to hopeful thoughts that it might even put in to Plymouth on the way up the Channel. The cost was £46 each, to be collected from my father in England.

Frenzy set in. The heavy trunks had to be dispatched ahead to the

Hoboken Pier to go in the hold for the voyage carefully labelled "Not Wanted on Voyage". One great advantage of going from here was that this was in the state of New Jersey straight across the River Hudson from Manhattan Island and thus not so far from Moorestown. This was helpful because it meant we would not have to spend a night nearer the ship but could make the journey to embarkation on the day of departure. Then news came through that the sailing was delayed three days until the afternoon of 23rd August, five years to the day from when we arrived in Montreal.

One of my mother's last events was to attend the Moorestown Quaker Monthly Meeting and the meeting for worship that preceded it. Here she had the opportunity to thank the Quaker community once more for all they had done for her daughters. She always became very nervous doing this, but knew she had to do it. It was her duty to do so. Speaking in Meeting is a very personal matter and she would become self-conscious when she did. Father had written saying how important it was for her to thank the Americans sincerely, once again, for all they had done. As is the custom when Friends move from one Meeting to another she was given a Minute to take home to her Monthly Meeting in Plymouth acknowledging these events.

Last minute shopping was crammed in. Last good-byes said to all our friends and adopted relations, Uncle Charlie given his last leaving present, the covered wagon I had made, "Tobo or Bust", as a special memento of all the times I had enjoyed with him during my stay. Our day for leaving was getting closer by the minute.

Just before we left Mother had a birthday. Would all her birthdays from now on be associated with our going to America and our return so near this day? My present to her was some tapestry for a Tobo chair seat that I had brought with me when we came and had now managed to finish it at last, five years later, and it too was going home to Tobo, packed into the luggage.

Six of us climbed into the car to go to Hoboken Pier. Aunt Nancy, Anne, Richard and we three Lawsons. There had been an awful worry in the last few weeks because Anne had been away visiting some cousins and we could not have borne to have left without saying good-bye to her if she had not been back in time. She after all had been our carer in so many ways, teacher and originator of endless games and activities more than any other member of the family, very important to Blanche and me.

We arrived at the quay side to find crowds of people thronging around, all in a high state of excitement trying to find uniformed porters in their distinctive red caps to help manhandle the luggage aboard the liner whose side was towering over the whole proceedings like the side of a cliff. The gang planks sloped up to holes in the side of the boat where people were disappearing into the interior. We followed our luggage aboard up one of these to see where our cabin and home for the next nine days was going to be.

The *Nieuw Amsterdam* had just come off troop ship duties and the cabin we found was suitably accommodated. It was equipped with seven three-tier bunks in a cabin which in peace time would have housed perhaps three people. Luckily, we discovered we were not to have twenty-one people like the soldiers, only nine of us were crowded in together. Having established our sleeping quarters we returned to the shore with the Woods where we now all stood with nothing left to say awaiting the final call of "All Aboard".

"Aunt Nancy, you will find Sherry a good home if you can't keep her," I begged

"Joan you will be met in Southampton by Francis, won't you?" Aunt Nancy asked. "He will be back from Guernsey by now, won't he?"

"Mother", asked Blanche, "What is going to happen about school for me?"

We knew all the answers to these questions, everything had been gone over lots of times already, we really had nothing left to say. Eventually I could bear it no longer and flung myself into Anne's arms and burst into tears. It was all too distressing. This was the trigger and soon the whole party was weeping. How tragic for all of us it was. Little did we realise the problems ahead.

CHAPTER THIRTY-EIGHT

Homecoming

THERE WAS AN INEVITABILITY about our leaving America. I knew it had to happen but that did not make it any easier. By nature an optimistic and cheerful person this was a quite daunting and heart wrenching event. I remember it with much greater grief than I do of leaving England in 1940. My mother still seemed a stranger compared to the now loved and familiar Aunt Nancy. Nine days at sea at least was going to give us a period of adjustment to each other.

ATLANTIC CHALLENGER.—The Nieuw Amsterdam, a Dutch challenger for Atlantic supremacy, now at Southampton, carried many British Service men when on trooping duties in the war.

The Nieuw Amsterdam

There is lots of excitement when a large liner leaves harbour. The *Nieuw Amsterdam* was about the fifth in size of all the magnificent ships that crossed the Atlantic in splendour before the outbreak of War. Despite the rather tired look of her now, after five years of carrying servicemen around the world, she still was of such an impressive size that no one could but be impressed by all the excitement as she made ready to depart the Hoboken Quay.

So we blinked back our tears, leaned on the rail and waved frantically to the Woods still left on the quayside looking very small from our great height. When would we see them again? What was it going to be like back in England once more? One compensation was that we would see Daddy and brother John again. Would they seem as strange as Mother did when she arrived in Moorestown? I was sailing off into a sea of questions.

It took a while to pull the gang planks ashore and loosen the mooring lines so we could get under way. The wonder at the size of those ropes needed to hold such a gigantic ship. The small figures on the quayside began drifting away and we waved our final waves to the rumble of the deep throated engines as the tugs began pulling the ship out into the Hudson River so she could make her way out to sea. The hooter rang out the blasts signalling to other ships our intention to leave harbour. Sedately we sailed down the river passed the end of Manhattan Island with all its skyscrapers including the spot where the twin towers of the World Trade Center would eventually stand and then passed the Statue of Liberty into the Atlantic Ocean. I watched New York being left astern. Good bye America.

We were finally on our way home. I soon got used to life aboard ship. Mother and Blanche were appalled to find the troops had left us some souvenirs of their travels in our bunks in the form of bedbugs. A diligent inspection and massacre dealt with their presence and we got used to our cramped quarters.

The Pickards, Bertram, Irene and their daughter Erica who was a little older than Blanche, had joined us after all. Bertram was a friend of Uncle Dick's who worked for a Quaker organisation in Geneva. I had met him in Moorestown and, following that visit, he had written, in April 1944, to my mother reporting on our successful adjustment into the Wood family adding percipiently that perhaps as a mother the news of having someone usurping her place with her daughters would be received with mixed feelings.

Another Friend on board was Horace Alexander who was what I would call a "weighty" Friend. In my vocabulary this meant he was respected among Friends but with a certain lack of humour and certainly unused to talking with young girls such as me. Not surprisingly this little group of Friends tended to keep together during the voyage. Horace and Mother amused themselves with long discussions about the state of the world and he would also regale us with how he had met Ghandi when he was in India. I considered him very old but realise that he was no older than my mother, just touching forty. He seemed very middle-aged to me.

Fortunately this time there was little or no sea sickness and we entertained ourselves with games and books as well as getting exercise by walking around the promenade deck, four times around made a mile. Card games were a good way of passing the hours until a gust of wind took some cards overboard and ruined the pack. All this done to the continuing sound of the engines as they churned the ocean waters out behind the stern taking us steadily further from America.

Our first close view of England was early in the morning when the *Nieuw Amsterdam* turned into the Solent. The engines changed their tune as they slowed down and tugs came to guide us to our berth. A hurried breakfast and last things put into cases, then back on deck to lean over the side and watch as the large liner was manoeuvred alongside. Way down on the quay were crowds of upturned faces.

"I can't see them," I announced. "Can you, Blanche?"

"Look, there they are," said Mother, "and they have Grandpa with them. Oh, how glad I am to see your Father again. I have really missed him so much while I have been away. At long last I am going to have all my family together again."

We waited our turn to disembark, with porters once more to help with the luggage but not as colourful as the American ones who had helped us aboard. I recognised Daddy all right, the same soft spoken loving father we had left behind but John was now a fair haired little boy of eight quite unlike the toddler we had left behind. He in his turn could not remember us at all but only knew of us from his parents talking about us. At one point he had even questioned if we even existed at all. Now seeing us he at least knew we were real. He told me later that he wondered if I was an American Indian I was so dark and tanned from a summer playing outdoors in the New Jersey sun and even doubted I was his sister.

Daddy and Grandpa had arrived in two cars, a little black Austin 7 that was my father's and a beige coloured Austin 10 that was Grandpa's. Luckily they had been able to hoard enough petrol to make the 300 mile trip from Plymouth to Southampton and back. It helped that as growers and farmers they had more flexibility with the petrol ration than others might have. There were six of us and our luggage to make the journey. The heavy trunks in the hold would come on by railway.

By now it was lunch time and we had to find somewhere to eat. We finally found a cafe that was still serving. That meal was a revelation! The first course was macaroni cheese and cabbage followed by lumpy macaroni pudding for dessert, as we Americans always called it. Is this what English food was like now? I was assured that it wasn't usually quite as bad as this. Oh, for Aunt Nancy's cooking.

We were soon to learn what food shortages and rationing actually meant. We would have white bread that was grey, powdered eggs, very little butter and sugar and meat that was strictly limited; even candy was rationed. It had been back in 1941 I had had the idea of sending butter to England so I was aware of the problems in England but the reality was quite different. Here is a list of what it was for one person:

WEEKLY RATIONS in 1945
2oz. butter
2oz. cheese
1 egg
1 packet dried eggs
4oz. margarine /cooking fat
4oz.bacon/ham

2–3 pints milk

8oz. sugar

3oz.sweets

2oz. tea

meat

Unlimited vegetable, fruit, fish, bread and oatmeal

It was a long journey home up hill and down hill through the rural countryside of Dorset and Devon. The best part for me was that Blanche and I took turns to ride with Daddy in the baby Austin and talk to him. He was easy to talk to and listened to me talking about my life in America and told me what to expect now I was back in England. I was expected at a Friends boarding school in Somerset at the beginning of term which was hardly two weeks away.

We arrived back at Tobo to be met by a big tea all ready prepared for us by a friend of mother's. This was a "high" tea and certainly better than the lunch in Southampton. "High" tea is a very English institution, quite different from any meal we had had in Moorestown. Usually eaten early in the evening, it starts with a main course of meat and accompaniments of salad or vegetables followed by bread and butter and cakes or, if in Devon, scones with clotted cream and jam. This particular meal was the result of hoarded rations being eaten in one sitting but at least it made up for that dreadful lunch.

Seeing Tobo again brought back many memories. It and the garden definitely seemed smaller and many things were different too because the War had changed so many aspects of life in Britain. On first arrival Blanche and I had rushed around everywhere recognising things we remembered and noticing the changes.

Nevertheless, much was the same; the living room had the same furniture and rugs and rattly doors. The kitchen suddenly seemed very old fashioned compared to American kitchens, not even a fridge for instance. There were few changes, partly because things had had to last for the duration of the War. Often it was the little things that would trigger memories, like the carvings of animals up the staircase that had been done by my Father when the house was being built.

Now I was to have the luxury of a room to myself as were Blanche and John. Before I left Blanche and I had shared a room because then we had a live in maid who helped in the house and looked after us as well. I was to have the room at the back over the kitchen. It was an advantage to be over the warm kitchen because Tobo had no central heating and the extra warmth coming up through the floor in winter was most welcome. I took no time in putting up the ornaments I had brought back with me to remind me of America.

CHAPTER THIRTY-NINE

Back again at Tobo

THERE WERE MORE CHANGES in the garden because much of it had been dug up to grow vegetables, including the tennis court in Grandpa's garden next door. In the orchard across the road were ducks that were kept for their eggs and had to be fed every day on boiled-up potato peelings and other leftovers from the kitchen. It was an apple tree from this orchard that I remember drawing in my first letter home. The other orchards were at Dodovens where Father would go daily to get the milk.

"Daddy," I begged; "Do take me to see Dodovens, I want to see the cows. It's really exciting to think you have some cows. If you can keep a cow perhaps we could keep a horse?" I suggested. Father had bought the cows to ensure a good supply of milk for the house. Father amused us when he described the problems of keeping a house cow.

"Well, Lou I bought the cow when she was about to have a calf so when the calf came she would have plenty of milk for us as well. She was a good South Devon cow and she had so much milk that I had to buy another calf as well. As the calves got bigger we ran short of milk and I ended up buying another cow. By now as you see I have three cows and five calves and I don't quite know where it will all end."

The other livestock on this farm were the geese. I remembered well coming face to face with these geese especially the gander called Bill who could be very frightening. Sad to say Bill had departed in our absence, whether for a Christmas dinner or old age I never was told. Besides the milk, the cows made sure we could have the Devon clotted

Plymouth shopping centre before the war

cream which is so delicious and which we had enjoyed with that first tea at home. It is rather a long drawn out task making it. First the milk is stood for several hours, usually overnight, in a shallow bowl on a cold slab in the larder, then very slowly scalded so a rich crust of cream forms on the surface. Once again it is stood to cool and the last job is to carefully skim it off the surface, ready to eat. Unfortunately the skimmed milk left behind did not taste so good as ordinary milk.

As soon as we had returned home the following Sunday we went to meeting on Mutley Plain. It was a place that had not changed at all in either the building or the manner of worship. There were familiar faces there. The members of the Meeting were pleased to see us because they had been an important support to my parents all through our time away. What they thought of the two 'Americans' who had returned I can only guess.

Driving into Plymouth was an eye opener for now I could see (see p. 221) where the bombs had fallen and how the town had suffered.

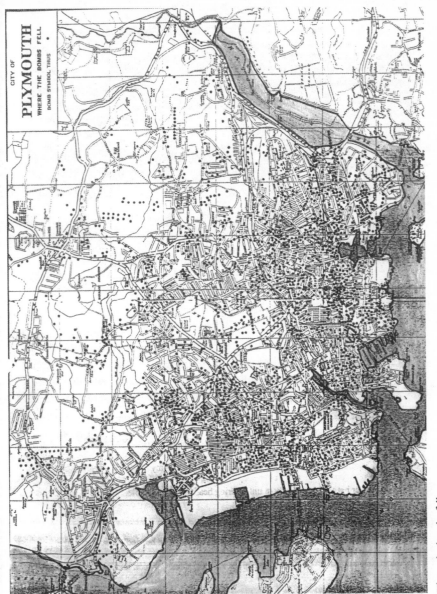

Where the bombs fell

Result of the bombing by 1945

Plymouth had been bombed severely so there were great areas where there were no proper buildings still standing, all that could be seen were just piles of rubble, roofless buildings and walls standing alone. You could come across a terrace of houses with gaps in between where one in the row had taken a direct hit, like a mouth with teeth missing. Sometimes you would see the inside walls of a house, showing the wallpaper and fireplace looking out into empty space.

Many of these bare spaces must have been there a long time because by now wild plants had established themselves in among the piles of debris. At the end of the summer it was the bright yellow ragwort and pink rosebay willow herb and purple buddleia that gave a splash of colour to this desolate landscape.

There was little time to enjoy the last of the school holidays because I had to be readied for boarding school and this meant buying the appropriate uniform.

There were practically no shops at all left in the city centre and they were managing by doing business in the front rooms of ordinary houses. I always wondered how my mother knew which house to go for which garments but she did and navy tunics with box pleats and of a certain regulation length just above the knee were bought. Once in school I soon discovered that short tunics were considered very little girlish and we tried hard to inch them lower, unlike a following generation in the 1960s who wanted it the other way and died to have them shorter.

Besides the tunic, were regulation navy knickers and knicker linings to go inside had to be bought to be worn underneath the tunic. In winter time you could add to these, lisle stockings that had to be held up with uncomfortable suspender belts. Thick woolly vests ensured warmth under a Viyella white blouse always worn with a school tie; no bra for me at this stage. School identification was the navy blazer with the school badge, a yellow ship on the pocket. Worst of all to my American eyes was the navy velour hat that was the most unflattering headwear imaginable.

All items had to be identified with name tapes that had to be hurriedly sewn on in the short time available. I had also been given a school number which had to go on as well. It was put on the bottom of my shoes in tacks. This number, 26, was mine for the whole of my school career and every peg I used whether in the changing room or locker was number 26.

CHAPTER FORTY

Sidcot School

S IDCOT FRIENDS SCHOOL, the boarding school where I was destined to go, is one of ten Friends Schools to be found in England. Sidcot was in Somerset, south of Bristol, beautifully situated in the country on the edge of the Mendip Hills over looking the Winscombe Valley. Though there has been a Quaker School here since 1699, in its present form it was founded in 1808 as a boarding school for boys and girls. It was one hundred miles from my home near Plymouth, so though it was the nearest such school, it did mean I had to be a boarder. Not a particularly large school, with around 100 girls and 100 boys, it was considered fairly progressive but not to the point of having no discipline or making lessons voluntary as more progressive schools did.

Central to the Quaker view on education is respect for the individual and a concern that pupils do not separate faith from practice in the way they treat each other. In other words you were taught to try and live by example in line with reverence for the life of all people

Sidcot School

in your community and the wider world aware that there is a strong potential for goodness in all people, deserving respect and dignity.

It amazes me that my parents having been without me for five long years felt it more important for me to go to a Quaker school than any alternative local school where I could live at home. Why did they do it? Certainly the climate of the times was that middle class children frequently went to boarding school and looking around my generation plenty of us did to which many biographies can attest. I doubt very much whether my parents even looked at local alternatives but I wonder if they realised the impact of this decision on our future relationship. Were they set on continuing to sacrifice their own desires for what they thought was the best for my education?

Looking back, now, and with the experiences of having three boys of my own, would I have done this? Probably not.

My mother had never been a hands-on mother in many ways. She had had a lot of help in caring for us before we went to America and my father had also taken a full share in looking after us, which was probably unusual for the time. He would regale us with tales of trying to get me to sleep in the middle of the night when I would wake up crying as a young child. Florrie, my adored nursemaid, had been brought in to allay these problems.

My mother, while I was very young, was hoping for a son and had suffered more than one miscarriage with this in mind. Thus, she had been told by doctors that she would have to take especial care if she was to succeed. It was at this time she developed the habit of an afternoon rest, which I have mentioned before, that she continued for the rest of her life. Hence, she passed a lot of care for my sister and me to others until my brother (and luckily it was a boy) was born in 1937, by which time I was at school.

This practice of giving our care to others is illustrated by an incident in my brother John's early life. When he was five or six months old he fell ill with pneumonia, a serious illness in those days, and he was very ill indeed. When the crisis came it was Mary Davies, the wife of Mutt Davies the Vinery lorry driver, who was helping in the house at the time who stayed up with John all night keeping him warm by the fire until the crisis was past. Mary successfully nursed him and he came through with no lasting effects.

While we were away in America I imagined that my brother would have been spoiled; perhaps he was, but he reports that care continued to be at the hands of maids until he went to nursery school. Then when he reached the age of six he was sent to a small boarding school in Plymouth already evacuated to Dartmoor. My mother would then have had no children at home at all and even during holiday times John spent a lot of time at the Vineries under the watchful eye of someone such as the Vinery carpenter. All through his school days he spent many hours of his holidays with these kind men as they went about their work.

Were Blanche and I sent away because she was fearful of how she would be able to cope with these two lively American teenagers who were now her responsibility? She was aware that Aunt Nancy had found it prudent to send Blanche away to board at Westtown School during her last year in America. The added problem for Aunt Nancy, at that time – and mother could not claim this excuse – was her poor health which was sapping all her energy. I certainly think there was a strong element of apprehension in my mother about her ability to cope in this decision to send us away, conscious or unconscious, especially as she and Blanche were still very wary of each other. Another aspect of the situation was that my mother was now having to share her husband with my glamorous older sister and a lively young girl such as me, also looking for attention from my father.

Was there, also, a wish to instil some "good English discipline" into these girls of hers? I think so. She definitely felt we had fallen into careless ways by English standards, and was looking to someone else to make us English again as soon as possible. Needless to say Blanche and I were quite happy the way we were and if anything wanted to hang on to our Americanisms as long as we could.

I knew I would go to Sidcot. Blanche, on the other hand, because of her age had not been accepted there so she was sent to another Friends school, Ackworth, in the north of England where their efforts to bring her into line were quite unimaginable severe. Here the buildings were freezing cold with little heating, pupils were only allowed to change clothes and have a shower or bath once a week, and they sent all her dresses from America home because they were deemed unsuitable. They also wanted to cut her hair but she refused and changed the style and piled it on top of her head. After all her fun with boys at West-town she discovered here that the boys and girls were taught in separate lessons and no fraternizing was allowed.

The teachers were unsympathetic, as instanced by the maths teacher who chastised and ridiculed her for not being able to work out sums in pounds, shillings and pence. Was the teacher so ignorant she did not know that in America she had been dealing in dollars and cents? Blanche was miserable. My parents were forced to move her and persuaded Sidcot to take her. She came and joined me after Christmas 1945. Sadly when John was equally unhappy at school in his teens, they never moved him even though they knew my sister was so much happier once she had moved.

I was taken to Sidcot that first time in the car by my parents, with all the new uniform, plus a warm eiderdown for my bed, all squashed into a trunk and put in what I still called the trunk of the car. Subsequently, I always went by train to and fro. It was quite a complicated journey with two train changes on the way; one at Taunton and another at Yatton, and I came to know it very well. The last bit going home was always best as the train went all along the South Devon shore beside the bright red cliffs. Today no one would dream of allowing anyone to build a railway line there, but Brunel got away with it. It was a steam train in those days and the very last bit from South Brent to Plymouth was downhill and we would go at a rattling pace before arriving at North Road Station, Plymouth.

One of the most important aspects of my time at Sidcot was the fact that my mother's eldest sister, Helen, lived in the village next to the school. The first time we stopped there before I was deposited in school. It was she that I considered was most like Aunt Nancy when I had written home from Moorestown. Like my mother she was an excellent needlewoman and a strength in the local Women's Institute.

I had memories of Aunty Helen from before the War when their family had visited us in Devon and I had visited them at Winscombe. In particular, I remember learning to ride a two wheeled bicycle on the front lawn of the large brick built Victorian house called Hampden where she lived. She and Uncle Eric had five children and the youngest, Brian, was in his last year at Sidcot when I began. He seemed much older than me and even more importantly he was a School Prefect. It was a comfort to know that he and Aunty Helen were close by.

While Blanche was in Yorkshire I too was going through the trauma of adjusting to England and a new school. It was bound to be a difficult time wherever and whatever I had done; and difficult it was. However, my experiences for a number of reasons were better than my sister's.

When I arrived back from America there were letters from three of my future classmates welcoming me to Sidcot. They were going to "show me the ropes" when I arrived so I knew I would have someone who would explain the complex life of the school.

"First of all," one of them explained when I arrived, "don't be late for breakfast in the mornings or being in bed at night or you'll get into trouble. Once in bed there is no talking after lights out (though that depends a bit on who is on duty). Going off the 'Island' is out of bounds without permission." The 'Island' was the name given to the school buildings and land contained by roads on all sides making it a quite protected environment.

"The other thing, Lou, is the times you can go to the 'boys' side. It's not too bad. You can even go for walks with the boys at weekends if you want to, but you'll have to write it in the leave book when you do. We have to go for walks every Saturday and Sunday, rain or shine; though if it's Saturday at least we can go the village and buy things we need in the shops there and after that go and watch any games matches on the playing field."

My experiences at summer camp at least had been something similar to what I could expect at boarding school which probably helped a lot. I was to sleep in a dormitory with iron cots and just a small cupboard to keep any personal items all fairly impersonal. I do not remember that this was a worry to me.

Life now was dominated by bells; when to get up, another to summon you to breakfast, then came the bell for form period after breakfast with our form mistress, Miss Martin, then another bell to start lessons. I was to learn that it was the job of the Upper Fourth to ring this hand bell and in due course I was to take my turn at this job, swinging this big bell by hand in the girls' hall.

Due to the difference in English and American education even though I had been a reasonably able pupil in Moorestown I was still put in a year group below my age in the English school, so I was the eldest in the class. Luckily I was small and immature for my age so this was never a problem. Scholastically there were quite a lot of differences. The lessons I now had to do included French which I had never done and the class had already done a year. I don't think I ever did catch up. We were taught by Miss Jackson, a very spinsterish lady with hair pulled back in a severe bun who was generally known as "Ma Jack". Ma Jack was not an inspiring teacher and struggled to keep order and our interest. French was not a subject I could ever do.

I have already mentioned the troubles I had with changing from American to English both in matters of grammar and of spelling. English as taught in England seemed such a fastidious activity compared to how we learnt in America. Then there was trouble with history; I had only been studying American history and suddenly I found myself expected to know the dates of all sorts of treaties in Europe all through the 19th century. There was a great emphasis on learning those dates. These events I found very difficult to memorise or find relevant and again I was probably hampered by what the class had learnt the year before which may have given the lessons more relevance.

One of my main memories of my first weeks at Sidcot was when one of the boys arrived back late that term because he had had chicken pox.

"Lou, Iain wants to meet you," said one of my friends after we had finished prep one evening and amusing ourselves on the girls' side doing nothing in particular.

"Why should he want to see me?" I asked. I ran up stairs to the dorms to hide but they dragged me out to come down the long staircase to the girls hall below. The boys were at the bottom of the stairs all looking up when I was pushed to the front of the crowd.

"Go on say something," they all begged.

"Aw gee, what shall I say? " I asked in my broad American accent. I dare say I managed to say a little more than that. I realised then that I was deemed unusual, so once more I was the outsider and different from everyone else, sufficient of an oddity to be shown off by the rest of the class on this occasion. When would I be one of them?

There were many other aspects of my new life that were different. Reminders of the

Louise in 1946

deprivations that the War had brought was most noticeable in the food we had. Everyone had their own butter bowl and each week on Mondays we would get the meagre amount of butter that was our ration for the week. Was it two ounces? The butter bowls were not big but all identified by your own school number as were the boys' bowls. The boys had a similar numbering system but generally your "opposite" was in a different class and as we sat in our classes boy girl, boy girl, there wasn't often confusion. Personalities could be identified depending whether you hoarded your supply for breakfasts and bread and butter teas or found the whole supply had gone by Wednesday

General food shortages meant we were filled up with tapioca puddings, spotted dick and blancmange, usually of a lurid pink colour. The prefect at the end of the long table dished out the courses for us. I soon learnt to eat at speed to ensure a second helping before supplies had run out. One thing we did that autumn to help the food situation was for the whole school to be sent out blackberry picking. The school was right in the country so it wasn't difficult for us to find the ripe fruit in the hedgerows nearby. Like most blackberry picking it came with the usual hazards of stinging nettles and sharp brambles so enthusiasm could wane even though there was a prize for the class that picked the most. I remember some in the class, and we had all gone together, became rather fed up with it all and changed from picking the berries to smearing the blackberry juice over their faces so they really looked like Red Indians by the time we got back. I looked on in wonder at this childlike activity and began to realise that the discipline at the school was going to have a certain flexibility.

Like all new schools, the first weeks were really hard, it was all so unlike Moorestown. I was having to make new friends. It turned out that my mentors who had kindly cared for me during the beginning of term were not going to become my closest friends, partly because they were in different sets for lessons and with different interests. Much of the time we sat alphabetically in our form rooms and I became friends with the girls who were my alphabetical neighbours, Rosie Lambert and Veronica Newbery on either side of Lawson. Even though we had lessons with the boys at that stage I still tended to sit with other girls.

However, like going to America, there was one aspect that was the same. This was the Quakerism that was the fundamental basis of the school philosophy and of the people with whom I found myself. In particular we had an outstanding Headmistress, Miss Hooper, commonly known as "Poppy". My mother in a moment of wisdom was aware that I would perform better where I respected the Headmistress; everyone respected Poppy, myself included. She was approachable and fair. She always impressed us by the stillness with which she sat through the Sunday Quaker Meetings an example to us all on how to calmly sit, meditate and reflect on one's daily life.

Over the next five years we would come to know each other well. It was not unusual for me to find myself outside her door awaiting a telling off for some misdemeanour or mischief and the approach was not unlike Aunt Nancy.

"Well, Louise, what have you got to say for yourself? Does your conscience not tell you that this is not the right behaviour. You should know better. Now go away and behave yourself, I don't want to have you sent to me again, please."

Miss Hooper was a guiding light through all my time at school. I was sufficiently in awe of her to accept her judgments but knew that if there were any problems she would be the best person to go to. Her wisdom sorted out skilfully the friendship changes that seem to be the trial of girls at school, who is or is not your best friend and the repercussions for everyone as the liaisons altered.

Aunty Helen also became an important person in my life during my time at Sidcot and particularly in those early days. Frequently I would find myself seated on the floor in front of a lovely open fire making toast with bread balanced on the end of a toasting fork for Sunday afternoon tea, sometimes with one of my new friends. I would have met her after morning Meeting to arrange the visit. She was an eminently practical person, not particularly demonstrative but always there and reliable. Better still, I do not remember her ever making a comment on my American accent, I was accepted for who I was, not who I might have been.

Even though a visit to Aunty Helen would mean I was excused the Sunday afternoon walk, I learned a love of walking and the countryside while I was at Sidcot. In my early days the walks may well have only been in the fields behind the school in the Coombe, later they would extend to the top of nearby Mendip hills such as Wavering Down, Crooks Peak or even further a field to Blackdown.

I began to settle in and this was where my prowess at hockey came to my aid. Within a few weeks I was playing in the first eleven hockey team and suddenly life got better. I was able to wear a much cherished yellow girdle with my school tunic. Whether my new school friends resented this rise in my fortunes I do not remember, perhaps some did, but others did not or else I was too pleased with the fun of the game to mind. From then on sport was my greatest love; whether hockey, swimming, tennis or gym I just rejoiced in it all.

CHAPTER FORTY-ONE

Christmas 1945

B Y T H E T I M E I G O T home for the Christmas holidays I was becoming a little more used to life in England. School routine included always writing letters home on Sunday mornings before Meeting which meant my parents had some idea of what was happening during my life at school. I soon learnt how this information could be controlled. Thus they would always be told the result of yesterday's hockey match, who it was against, what the score was and how much I had enjoyed it. Since I played half-back, who shot the goals was not included information until Blanche came and joined me in the team and as she was a forward she could include that bit. My mother would complain about the over emphasis on hockey which I considered not very supporting because I enjoyed it above all other activities.

I also learned to filter out information about which boy I had been for a walk with last Sunday and generally keep their eyes off my social life with the opposite sex. I discovered over the years that it didn't matter who it was, there would only be critical comments. Mother, unlike many Friends, was not particularly good at seeing the "good" in others and especially not in my boyfriends! Even my husband who was charming, successful and a very good husband and father, can never remember receiving a compliment from that quarter. I discovered, too, that my American "difference" made me attractive to the boys so I certainly made the most of it.

This thought makes me wonder how much all those other letters across the Atlantic were written with what the correspondent wanted the recipient to hear in mind. My belief is that Aunt Nancy, as an honest person, was as honest as she could be, though playing down some of the family frictions occasionally as well as some of the difficulties.

Interestingly, my mother also wrote her weekly letters to the school on Sunday and though it meant I would be certain to get a letter on a Monday morning it did mean that dialogue was restricted because it would be another week before a reply might come to questions I might ask. My mother's inflexibility was not helping us to establish a close relationship; after all I was restricted by the school timetable – she surely could have found another slot in the week in which to sit and write letters to her children.

Once we had left Moorestown Aunt Nancy stopped writing. I imagine that she wished us to have a clean break so we could re-establish ourselves in England without harking back to our American lives. Anne has told me subsequently that once we had gone "there was no grieving", which is hard to understand. I would have expected as great emotional involvement towards us as we had toward the Wood family. Blanche and I both consider the care we had during those five years was decisive in our development.

Aunt Nancy always considered caring for us her "War Work"   and once the war was over she had completed her task. This though is an over-simplification. We were much too involved one with another to walk away so easily. In some ways it could be compared to a teacher when her class leaves school, life carries on. Again not quite as simple as that. I know I regretted not hearing very much but in a way accepted that I had to get on with my English life.

There are no letters kept from the Wood family that first year after we got back. However, there is one interesting letter from my much loved mentor, Uncle Charlie, dated 26th November 1945 strangely enough to my mother. Was there a policy decision within the family in America not to distress us by writing to us? It would almost suggest there was.

Charles Evans
Riverton, N.J.

Dear Friend,
Joan Lawson
I think that Louise, who has written me a charming letter from Sidcot, would like me to send her a horse for Christmas, unfortunately I am no judge of horseflesh and there is the difficulty of transport. So for the present I am subscribing to the National Geographic Society's monthly publication which I have directed to be sent to Tobo as I was not sure Louise would be at Sidcot for a twelvemonth. I hope it will not be a nuisance for you to send it on. We had another shameful turkey dinner on Thanksgiving at Richard Wood's and often thought of Blanche, Louise and yourself.

Nancy allowed me to read your letter which gave so much information as to the situations at Ackworth and Sidcot etc. We also saw Blanche's letter to Anne Wood which was quite interesting.

Nothing much happens here 'we plow along as the fly said to the ox, half the time on foot and the other half walking'; but all the family is well and far warmer than I fear you are.

Our house is being painted, a great nuisance, but an operation much needed, as one visitor said it is to be hoped the paint will stay on longer than the smell. I was fortunate in obtaining real lead and oil, the cost of labour is now very high.

Louise says in one letter, not to me, to send her something to eat. If I do send her a fruit cake and she then gets sick should I be blamed? If I do send something of the kind I shall recommend homeopathic doses. I expect the child is generally hungry, you know she always was.

With every good wish for the holidays and much later,
  Your friend,
    Charles Evans

Certainly this letter suggest there was correspondence but not a lot.

A special effort was made to make this an enjoyable Christmas in the same way a special effort was made that first Christmas I had at 272. Though I may have made some presents at school as I had frequently done before, I certainly will have had little opportunity to buy presents while at school so there was a mad rush of present buying once I got home. Fortunately there was my grandfather's shop where things could be bought at a discount which was a useful source of gifts even at this stage of post war austerity. In those days it included a toy department where I could be sure of finding a suitable dinky car for John or something for the kitchen for Mother. In later years I would find myself behind the counter of the toy department helping out and earning some extra money. It could be pandemonium in the days before Christmas.

There were other Christmas activities once we returned, centred on the Swarthmore Friends Meeting in Plymouth. We went carol singing, even though I was quite useless at singing and was generally out of tune. The opportunity was used to raise money for a worthy cause. Sidcot was a musical school and I had realised during that first term how musical were many of my classmates, being participants in choirs and orchestras. My earlier efforts at violin playing were sufficient reminder that my talents lay elsewhere.

We had German Prisoners of War, who had yet to be repatriated now that hostilities were over, for Christmas tea. The P.O.W.s had been working at Dodovens Farm and the Vineries and were experiencing yet another Christmas away from home. Father had got to know one or two of them quite well, particularly their pastor. Besides singing "O Tannenbaum" around the piano while Mother played we had also played "Up Jenkins".

"Up Jenkins" is a simple game which can be great fun. Two teams sit opposite each other across the dining room table. One team has a sixpence which must be concealed in their hands from the other side. The game starts when the first team passes the sixpence from hand to hand under the table and on the order 'Up Jenkins' from the other team must place their clenched hands on the table. The second team leader can now tell them to do any of three things in the effort to find who is hiding the sixpence between their fingers. These are Creepy Crawly (fingers moving by crawly movements forward on the table), Wibbly Wobbly (clenched hands to be turned over and back on the table), and

Flat on Table (hands to be laid flat on table). Meanwhile the opposing team listens for a tell tale clink as the coin will slip and hit the table.

This produced much hilarity amongst the P.O.W.s because their work worn hands were quite clumsy and then there was the added problem of explaining what wibbly wobbly was in German.

Earlier in the day we had opened our presents. Luckily we girls were not yet considered too old to hang up our stockings. Though they were not elaborately filled, we enjoyed finding useful things like hairgrips, toothpaste or soap as well as a precious orange and nuts at the toe. Even some chocolate from the sweet ration.

Father was a great one for heightening the excitement of the festive season by teasing us all about what presents we were going to get.

"You know, Lou, I wonder if you can guess what you're going to have for Christmas? It has black and white stripes! What do you think that will be?"

"It's a bicycle," I would guess. "Or is it a zebra?"

"No, try again." I would rack my brain for what it could be.

We had to wait for the black and white stripes until after breakfast was over and cleared. Daddy and John disappeared and Blanche and I were kept indoors to await a surprise. What could it be?

Blanche and I were led outdoors and around the corner of the house came a pony and trap with John dressed up as Father Christmas holding the reins. Just what I was longing for, a real Dartmoor pony. Oh what true delight! A brindled grey pony (hence the black and white stripes) called Maisie, with the softest light grey muzzle and a lovely gentle temperament. She was not very big, about 12 hands high, but big enough for me to ride as well as ride behind her around the lanes in the trap. She, and later a slightly larger pony, which we got later on, appropriately called Tinker because he really was a bit of a Tinker, gave Blanche and me excitement and activity which would make up for our great loss having left our happy life with the Wood family.

CHAPTER FORTY-TWO

End piece

A S THE YEARS WENT by I knew without doubt that my sojourn in America had more positive outcomes than negative. I have benefited remarkably from the whole experience. Even though my relationship with my mother suffered, my eventual happiness at Sidcot School and the years that followed have been full of good fortune. I enjoyed my time at University and was lucky to meet my husband there. My character was strengthened by the whole episode. By nature a cheerful and optimistic person, having to cope with adversity early in life meant I learnt to cope with difficulties all through my life when they occurred.

I remained a dutiful daughter. My father was accepting and did his best to smooth over Mother's excesses of behaviour. My mother, spoilt as the youngest of her family of six, was indulged by first her own father and then by my father and was used to having her own way. However, in this particular situation many events were well beyond her control, her own wishes could not be realised. She always regretted the consequences of the decision she and my father made to send her daughters away and tried hard to erase the American influence of which she was so jealous. She was not prepared to wait for the Americanisms to fall away naturally.

There is no doubt that the greatest loser in this whole story was my mother. She missed out on seeing her daughters grow and develop at a critical time. Sadly she was not able to accept my sister and me as we were when we returned as my father and Aunty Helen did and thence

The Wood Family 1946, Becca, Aunt Nancy, Uncle Charlie and Anne, Richard in front with Dora

Uncle Dick and Aunt Nancy visiting England in 1952

gradually establish a new relationship with us.

As a teenager when home from boarding school I would challenge her, often successfully, so over the years she was more circumspect in her behaviour towards me, more so than to my sister whom she would treat really unkindly at times. My school friends in England have reminded me that I would 'warn' them of my mother's sharp and critical tongue when they came to visit to ensure they would not take her barbed comments too personally.

In boarding school one looked to one's peers for support and in the caring community of Sidcot I got support from other pupils and teachers which I might have expected from my parents in other circumstances. This, and the presence of Aunty Helen near at hand, enabled me to slowly become Anglicised despite myself. However, the basic ethics of the Society of Friends taught me throughout my childhood have stood me in good stead.

From my earliest contact with Uncle Charlie it was no surprise that

Louise and Richard, in England 2002

my field of study at University was first geography, geology and botany in a general degree followed by a geology honours degree. I was perhaps ahead of my time as a woman geologist so my first job was involved with land use (agriculture and planning) in the West of England. This lasted only a short while before I married Graham Milbourn, a fellow student at Reading University, who became a successful agricultural scientist first as a university lecturer and professor and then the director of a scientific research institute in Cambridge, the National Institute of Agricultural Botany. Later I became a teacher of geography and geology in boys' secondary schools in Kent, Edinburgh and Cambridge. Now in retirement I chair the Cambridgeshire Geology Club and have been chairman of governors of our nearby secondary school.

I have continued to have contact with my "American Family". Once travel became a little easier after the war visits to and fro across the Atlantic in both directions took place. For me any contact was like a home coming. The most memorable was when I took Graham, our family of three sons (11, 8 and 5 years old at the time) to meet the Woods for the first time. What a welcome we had! Richard and his wife, Bitsa, who had a family of four children around the same ages as ours was a dairy farmer in Maine. We camped in his farmyard in Maine while at the same time Aunt Nancy and Uncle Dick were staying in the house next door with Anne and Becca and her three children. The highlight of the visit was what was known as the four 'Gs' birthday party. This was to celebrate the birthdays of Gilbert, Richard's son, Geoffrey, Becca's son, Graham and Grandfather Wood (Uncle Dick). It was a grand occasion we all remember. To this day we remain in touch.

Graduation Day 4th July 1953 at Reading
University. Father, Louise and Mother